Introducing Globalization
Theories

Introducing Globalization Theories

A Concise Overview for Students

Manfred B. Steger

UNIVERSITY OF CALIFORNIA PRESS

University of California Press
Oakland, California

© 2025 by Manfred B. Steger

All rights reserved.

Library of Congress Cataloging-in-Publication Data

Names: Steger, Manfred B., author.
Title: Introducing globalization theories : a concise
 overview for students / Manfred B. Steger.
Description: Oakland : University of California Press,
 [2025] | Includes bibliographical references and index.
Identifiers: LCCN 2024041140 | ISBN 9780520389915
 (hardback) | ISBN 9780520389922 (paperback) |
 ISBN 9780520389946 (ebook)
Subjects: LCSH: Globalization—Study and teaching.
Classification: LCC JZ1318 .S7436 2025 | DDC 303.48/2071—
 dc23/eng/20241126
LC record available at https://lccn.loc.gov/2024041140

34 33 32 31 30 29 28 27 26 25
10 9 8 7 6 5 4 3 2 1

In memory of Lawrence Leon Besserman
(1945–2017)
brother-in-law, mentor, scholar

CONTENTS

List of Illustrations   ix

Preface and Acknowledgments   xi

Introduction: What Is Globalization Theory?

1

1. General Theories

38

2. Domain Theories

72

3. Complexity Theories

106

4. Critical Theories

138

5. New Theories

171

Brief Guide to Further Reading 205

Index 211

ILLUSTRATIONS

1. Theory and theorizing: The scientific method 3
2. Genealogy of "globalization" 9
3. Core concepts of globalization theory 18
4. Social imaginaries 21
5. Modes of theorizing globalization 31
6. Globalization and modernity: Giddens versus Albrow 58
7. David Held's general globalization theory 62
8. William Robinson's theory of global capitalism 82
9. Deterritorialization absolutists and relativists 88
10. Three theories of cultural globalization 98
11. Attributes of complexity theory 111
12. Saskia Sassen's global cities model: Seven complexity hypotheses 117
13. The new vocabulary of global complexity 133
14. Two stages of critical thinking 143

x / *Illustrations*

15. Characteristics and outcomes of critical globalization thinking 153
16. Global citizenship as a process 156
17. The Great Unsettling 176
18. Paul James and Manfred Steger's four globalization formations 185
19. Disjunctive globalization: Extensity 188

PREFACE AND ACKNOWLEDGMENTS

Although the term *globalization* appeared in the English language as early as the 1920s, it was not until the Roaring Ninety-Nineties that it took the world by storm. Popularly understood as expanding processes of economic interconnectivity fueled by the Information and Communication Revolution, the new buzzword elicited strong opinions and emotions among supporters and detractors alike. Global media corporations headquartered in the Global North acted mostly as globalization cheerleaders by leveraging their powerful position in the sprawling digital news networks to saturate the public discourse with benign images of the benefits of free trade and cheaper consumer goods. Billions of ordinary people around the world latched on to the neoliberal idea of globalization as beneficial market integration, hoping that they, too, would reap its material rewards in the not-too-distant future.

After enjoying a decade of popularity in the 1990s, globalization's reputation has suffered in the turbulent opening decades of the twenty-first century. Major disruptors of global connectivity included the surge of transnational terrorism starting with the 9/11 al-Qaeda attacks, the 2008 Global Financial Crisis and the ensuing Eurozone Debt Crisis, swelling global migration and refugee flows in the 2010s and 2020s, the 2020–23 COVID-19 pandemic, inflationary pressures, and intensifying geopolitical conflicts followed by major wars in Eastern Europe, Africa, and the Middle East.

The impact of this global destabilization alongside ingrained systemic challenges, such as climate change and economic inequality, has raised the specter of hyper-nationalism fueled by *deglobalization*. To be sure, some forms of global interconnectivity, like global supply chains and free trade, have come under significant strain in the 2020s and are currently being reconfigured. Still, other aspects of globalization, like social media networks and digital cultural flows, have been flourishing more than ever before. Hence, some observers object to the characterization of the present state of incipient globality as the *end of globalization*.

To be sure, globalization—and how to measure its many dimensions—has remained on contested and slippery theoretical terrain. While scholars often disagree on matters of definition, central features, impact, causality, and methodological approaches, most would concur that the term relates to the ongoing worldwide *compression of space and time*. This influential expression refers to the reduction of spatial barriers to movements, the annihilation of time, and the shrinkage of distances. This uneven and often disrupted compression of space and time constitutes a central theme that has been theorized across the social sciences and humanities. Globalization theorists, in particular, seek to develop better understandings of how social change happens across world-space and world-time. Their propositions, interpretations, explanations, and predictions

Preface and Acknowledgments / xiii

serve as informative accounts for students of globalization around the world.

But this welcome proliferation of globalization theories in our young century has been a mixed blessing. On the upside, it has decentered the conventional international studies research focus on the nation-state by paying greater attention to transnational flows, interconnectivities, mobilities, and imaginaries. Many globalization theorists have embraced the emerging transdisciplinary field of global studies that challenges insulated knowledge silos forged in the crucible of *Euro-American-centric educational systems*. Moreover, by focusing on concrete social issues, globalization theorists have provided legislators and public policy-makers with new blueprints for solving our planetary problems.

On the downside, the mushrooming of globalization theories during the last two decades has made it much harder for general readers to maintain an overview of the subject. At times, theoretical debates on the subject have become cacophonous, confusing, and too narrowly geared toward academic insiders. Students and educated nonexperts who stand to benefit most from gaining greater insights into the processes driving global interconnectivity often become alienated by what they perceive as dense and arcane theory talk. To be sure, intensifying globalization dynamics defy easy explanations. But their increasing complexity only amplifies the need to bring more explanatory clarity to the academic study of the subject.

Thus, perhaps the biggest challenge facing globalization theorists today lies in organizing the welter of relevant materials without losing newcomers in a confusing flurry of names, dates, works, concepts, methods, and approaches. Another crucial task is to devise accessible narratives that stimulate students and a

xiv / *Preface and Acknowledgments*

broader audience while retaining enough intellectual heft to capture and convey academically sophisticated perspectives and arguments. Finally, facilitating a better understanding of globalization theories goes far beyond its obvious descriptive and explanatory value. Analytical insights always intersect with normative worldviews and the challenge of developing moral positions. Hence, the perhaps noblest goal of this short volume is to sharpen students' value judgments to find answers to the most important ethical question: how does globalization improve and/or impair the lives of sentient beings on our planet?

Taking up these three basic challenges—organization, accessibility, and normative assessment—this book offers a *concise* and *critical introduction to major globalization theories* that have emerged in academic settings across the world. It explains in accessible language how these theoretical frameworks have been conceptualized and assembled by influential thinkers who employ *different modes of inquiry*. Ultimately, the book argues that *globalization theorists have produced original insights and helpful explanations* while at the same time *still exhibiting major shortcomings*. The critical task of tackling these remaining weaknesses requires not only the integration of non-Western knowledge systems and new ecological insights, but also the linking up of theoretical reflection with the pressing global problems of our fast-changing world.

Both the theoretical and practical stakes in this ongoing intellectual quest are high. Globalization theories are far from lifeless abstractions floating in some ethereal sphere of abstract thought. Our actions in this world are *always* mediated by our ideas and values. The resulting ideological commitments manifest as authoritative pronouncements, potent metaphors, and compelling stories, all of which should be potentially capable of

Preface and Acknowledgments / xv

responding to practical concerns. In turn, ideas about globalization are shaped by material forces such as economic production systems, technology, social and political institutions, culture, climate, and geography. This interplay of thinking about the global and acting locally provides the contested *glocal* terrain of this book.

I owe a significant intellectual debt to my colleagues and students at the University of Hawai'i at Mānoa. Nothing is more important in higher education than stimulating discussions with fellow academic travelers, no matter at which stage of their professional careers they find themselves. I am extremely grateful for the steady stream of innovative ideas and feedback provided by Professor Paul James, a dear friend and leading globalization scholar at Western Sydney University, Australia. The late social thinker Roland Robertson has been a wonderful friend and mentor who urged me to pay attention to changing forms of global consciousness just as seriously as global material transformations. I also value Dr. Tommaso Durante's constant reminders of the significance of the media, images, and new forms of digital visuality for globalization research. Tommaso's pioneering "Visual Archive Project of the Global Imaginary" can be found at www.the-visual-archiveproject-of-the-global-imaginary.com.

I have been fortunate to have received steady feedback from many academic colleagues, including the anonymous external reviewers of this book manuscript. For many years, numerous readers, reviewers, students, and audiences around the world have offered insightful comments in response to my public lectures and publications on globalization and social theory. I am deeply indebted to them for helping me to hone my arguments.

Reed Malcolm, Naomi Schneider, and Aline Dolinh, my editors at the University of California Press, have been genuine beacons of support and encouragement. I especially appreciate Naomi's patience and graciousness in granting me a significant extension of the manuscript delivery deadline. I want to thank my PhD student Kelly Duong for her excellent work in preparing the index for this book. Finally, as always, a deep gasshō goes to my soul mate Perle Besserman—thanks for your brilliant editorial support and creative suggestions! Many people have contributed to the making of this book. However, its remaining flaws and shortcomings are my sole responsibility.

INTRODUCTION

What Is Globalization Theory?

This introduction undertakes a preliminary inventory of the nuts and bolts of globalization theory. Our intellectual journey into the heart of our subject starts with a brief clarification of the meanings of *theory* and *theorizing* in the social sciences and humanities, especially as these concepts relate to globalization. The bulk of the introduction is taken up with a basic examination of some fundamental concepts, features, and frameworks of globalization theory. This discussion is followed by a short historical account of the academic evolution of globalization theory over the last few decades. This section highlights some persistent shortcomings of globalization theory, particularly its narrow entanglements in dominant Eurocentric knowledge systems. Our inventory of the basics of globalization theory concludes with a short chapter outline that prepares us for the journey ahead.

THEORY AND THEORIZING

How should we understand *theory* in "globalization theory"? The term is derived from the classical Greek word *theoria*, which translates as "contemplation," "observation," and "gaze." Its meaning originally carried both philosophical and religious connotations. A *theorist* in the ancient world might be a specialist in rational reflection on the world or a skilled mediator between human and divine realms. In the secular context of modern science, theory lost its religious dimension but retained its emphasis on rationalism as an organized set of logical and empirically testable propositions about a subject. In the public discourse, however, *theory* is often used pejoratively as an untested idea or uninformed guess that contrasts practical ideas that work in the real world.

Whether theories address natural or social phenomena, they are the outcomes of formal processes of *theorizing*. Modern natural science links theorizing to stages of rational thinking associated with the *scientific method*. The process begins with *abductive thinking*, which refers to the creative ability to come up with a new idea or question, often as a result of careful observation. It then proceeds to *deductive thinking*, which is the development of conjectures or hypotheses from the original question followed by a prediction. The final stage of scientific theorizing involves *inductive thinking*, which centers on the empirical testing of the prediction.[1]

The production of new scientific theories or the refinement of existing frameworks depends on the successful interlinking of the tested propositions, ideally without causing too much friction. The smaller the number of primary principles involved, the more refined becomes the theory.[2] Strong theories that withstand multiple testing become the building blocks of overarching conceptual models. Such *paradigms* provide the framework of what, for a time, becomes "normal science"—a body of knowledge and methodologies accepted and defended by the dominant community of researchers.[3]

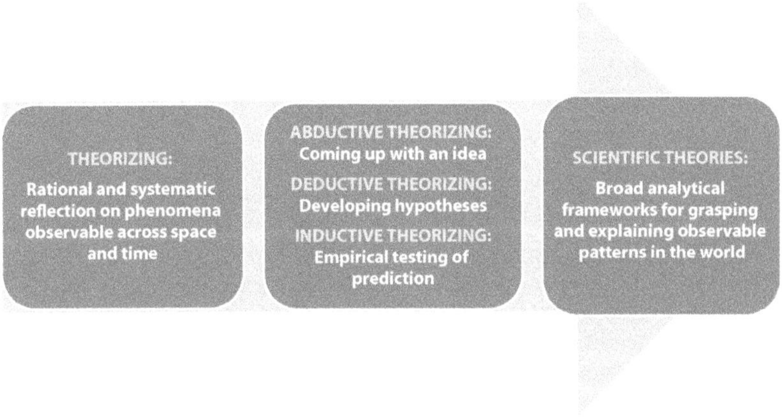

Introduction / 3

THEORIZING:
Rational and systematic reflection on phenomena observable across space and time

ABDUCTIVE THEORIZING: Coming up with an idea
DEDUCTIVE THEORIZING: Developing hypotheses
INDUCTIVE THEORIZING: Empirical testing of prediction

SCIENTIFIC THEORIES:
Broad analytical frameworks for grasping and explaining observable patterns in the world

Figure 1. Theory and theorizing: The scientific method

Natural and social phenomena are theorized at three connected levels of abstraction. *Macro-level theories* are made up of broad and abstract propositions about a patterned process such as globalization. They relate to large-scale issues and aim to be general enough to apply to different social and cultural contexts. *Mid-range theories* have a narrower research scope such as the economic or cultural dimension of globalization. While their lower level of generalizability reduces their range of applicability, it also allows for greater accuracy and explanatory clarity. *Micro-level theories* are narrowly focused on specific relationships between individuals and small social groups within a narrow social setting such as hospitals or universities.

Globalization thinkers with an affinity for the scientific paradigm pioneered in the natural sciences accept its premise that the validity of theories depends on the correspondence between their propositions (*logic*) and collected empirical facts and data (*evidence*) located in an allegedly *objective* external reality. Such a strong empirical focus, in turn, requires corresponding scientific theories to accommodate and organize relevant facts. Crucially, scientific theories must remain open to the possibility of error, meaning that hypotheses about globalization are subject to confirmation or falsification by hard data. Hence, the potential *refutability* of theoretical models is a necessary safety valve in the scientific process of making and revising knowledge claims based on empirical causal relationships.[4]

There exists, however, a long history of philosophical disputes about what counts as a *fact* and what constitutes *objective reality*. As emphasized in this book, globalization theorists embrace a variety of ways of making sense of the world becoming a more interconnected place. A good number of them have been uncomfortable with a scientific approach designed primarily to detect the causal mechanisms of globalization while staying away as much as possible from making value judgments or showing normative preferences. Such thinkers engage in a form of theorizing that involves deep *interpretation* of how *social meanings* about globalization are being formed and how they reflect and interact with specific norms and values embedded in competing political ideologies and clashing worldviews. Hence, the knowledge claims about globalization generated by such interpretive thinkers are less concerned with the scientific focus on objectivity and causality than with providing better understandings of the social constructions of our interdependent world.

Accordingly, interpretive thinkers tend to theorize globalization by employing suitable metaphors, narratives, analogies, and typologies. They tell a story of globalization in a normative language that is often at odds with the scientific idiom of *value-free* knowledge production.[5] Given the normative dimension inherent in social relations, interpretative forms of thinking often dovetail and overlap with *emancipatory* ways of reasoning that challenge existing social systems with the aim of bringing about more just social arrangements.[6] As we discuss in some detail in chapter 4, such normative theorizing calls for a close connection between critical theory and socially engaged practice.

To sum up, then, theories are the outcomes of systemic ways of theorizing that identify and analyze phenomena observable in space and time. Social theorizing proceeds at various levels of abstraction running from macro to micro. It can be scientific, interpretive, emancipatory, or a combination of these ways of reasoning. All of these approaches, however, seek to make sense of significant *patterns* in society.[7] The ability of researchers to recognize such patterns, and examine significant connections among them, depends on the cultivation of theoretical creativity and imagination. Innovative theorists are not afraid to think out of the box, even though it makes them more susceptible to the criticism, and even ridicule, of the guardians of dominant research paradigms.

GLOBALIZATION THEORY: THE BASICS

As noted in the preface, the main purpose of this book is to provide a concise introduction to influential globalization theories constructed by influential thinkers who cultivate distinct modes of theorizing. But before we turn to a discussion of these broad conceptual frameworks in the ensuing chapters, we have to get acquainted with some basic concepts and features of globalization theory that will prepare us for our journey into the heart of our subject.

Let us start out with a short description of the pertinent academic framework. Globalization processes are mostly theorized within and across the social sciences and humanities, which include the disciplines of sociology, anthropology, geography, history, literature, political science, urban studies, and others. Over the last three decades, the budding field of global studies has served as an intellectual incubator of much theorizing about the global. Indeed, the very concept of globalization itself is being continuously interrogated and contested. Relevant debates have yielded multiple disagreements as well as some agreements.

Crucially, most global studies scholars recognize that complex global interdependencies cannot be sorted out by specialists operating within the narrow confines of a single academic field. Hence, the field incorporates *transdisciplinary* and *multidisciplinary* approaches. Finally, global studies both embraces and exudes a holistic mindset, which I have called the *global imaginary*.[8] This core concept of globalization theory refers to a deepseated sense of the social whole as a worldwide community shaped by the intensifying forces of globalization. The growing power of the rising global imaginary goes a long way in explaining why global studies programs, departments, research institutes, and professional organizations have sprung up in most major universities around the world, including in the regions of the Global South.[9]

The designations *globalization theory* and *global theory* are often used interchangeably in academic discourse. Indeed, there exists considerable conceptual and thematic overlap. Both frameworks are designed to theorize globalization in modern societies. But there are also some significant differences. Most importantly, globalization theory focuses on the *flows of people, things, organizations, and ideas* across interconnected spatial scales running from the local to the global. Thus, it identifies as its basic unit of analysis interconnections and mobilities that operate across many

Introduction / 7

social dimensions and on multiple spatial scales. By contrast, global theory attends primarily to dynamics confined to the *global scale* such as emerging forms of global governance, transnational corporations, global supply chains, global music trends, global civil society actors, global communications networks, and so on.

International relations theory (IR theory), too, explores various transnational phenomena. Used primarily by political scientists and international studies scholars, IR theory tends to see the world through the lenses of *methodological nationalism*, which are focused on nation-states as the principal actors on the world stage. Unsurprisingly, globalization theorists have criticized mainstream IR thinkers for remaining stuck in outdated national frameworks. Some of them have expanded their criticism to the social sciences in general for failing to keep up with the ways in which globalization has weakened conventional forms of national sovereignty. To better understand the impact of the rapid increase in the scale and scope of human interactions, they argue, we need to make a global turn. This call has increasingly been answered, and the ensuing conceptual and methodological shift has begun to unsettle nation-centered perspectives.[10]

This book combines key approaches and insights from both globalization theory and global theory. IR theory only features in our discussion through the contributions of unorthodox IR thinkers who have turned against the prevailing methodological nationalism of their field and instead embraced the *methodological globalism* or *methodological glocalism* associated with global studies.

We are now ready to continue our inventory of globalization theory with a brief consideration of *basic definitions of core concepts*, *qualitative attributes*, and *quantitative measurements*.

8 / *Introduction*

Basic Definitions of Core Concepts

Before the late 1980s, *globalization* made but rare appearances in the English language.[11] While the meanings of seminal keywords such as *economics, culture,* or *modernity* evolved rather slowly and built upon a relatively continuous meaning base, *globalization* has had a rather short and discontinuous history, which involves a multiplicity of intellectual entry points and influences. Indeed, the meaning formation of globalization was many-branched. The genealogical findings in this introduction reveal the existence of at least four major trajectories in the explicit meaning formation of the concept from the late 1920s to the 1990s. The first meaning branch of the family tree called *globalization* is associated with the academic fields of education and psychology, the second with sociology and cultural studies, the third in politics and international relations (IR), and the fourth in economics and business.

Today *globalization* has become a keyword in public and academic discourse. Keywords are pivotal terms that carry influential meanings. They link meanings to important social relations and generate a set of related core concepts.[12] In the case of globalization, the most important related core concepts are *global, glocal, global imaginary, globality,* and *globalism.*

But to arrive at an initial definition of globalization, let us take a deeper look into the linguistic components of the keyword.

A simple grammatical breakdown yields two constitutive parts: *global* and *-ization.* The suffix is relatively easy to pin down. After all, the tacking on of *-ization* to adjectives is a common linguistic practice reflected in other important terms such as *modernization, industrialization,* and *bureaucratization.* They signify a process or series of actions or dynamics evolving slowly or

Introduction / 9

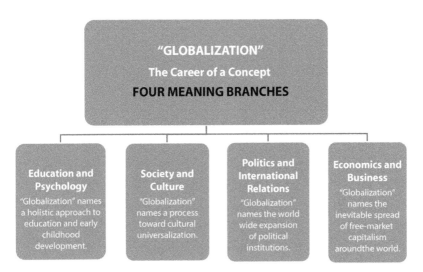

Figure 2. Genealogy of "globalization"

quickly in discernible patterns. Thus, *-ization* in globalization refers to the unfolding of global interdependencies in detectable patterns.

The adjective *global* in globalization, however, represents a much tougher semantic nut to crack. This core concept defies easy grammatical clarifications and thus requires a more elaborate explanation. For starters, we should note that *global* is a *spatial* term. It signifies "worldwide" or "involving and affecting the whole world." The word is rooted in the noun *globe*, which, in turn, derives from the Latin *globus*, referring to a rounded object.

As early as the third century BCE, ancient Greek astronomers established the roughly round shape of Earth as a physical fact by calculating our planet's circumference to an astonishingly accurate degree. Their representation of world-space as *sphaira* (Greek for "orb" or "ball") diffused quickly across the Mediterranean region and penetrated as far as India. At the time, other civilizations articulated very different spatial imaginations of the world. For example, Mesopotamian astronomers conceived of the world as a layered cosmic mountain. Chinese philosophers envisioned a flat disk floating in a vast ocean with a hemispherical sky-dome hovering above. Contrary to popular stories that cast medieval Europeans as believers in a flat world, ancient Mediterranean knowledge of Earth's spherical shape never disappeared from the region. In fact, it guided the navigational efforts of Christopher Columbus, Ferdinand Magellan, and other sixteenth-century agents of expanding European empires eager to reach Asia by way of the Atlantic Ocean.

First attempts to fashion a material model of Earth as a spherical object resulted in the construction of a twenty-inch terrestrial *globus*. The project was commissioned in 1490 by the German cartographer and commercial traveler Martin Behaim. The obvious omission of "America" was corrected in 1507 by a new globe created by the German cartographer Martin Waldseemüller. Still, it took until 1543 to refute the classical thesis that the world's surface was divided into two separate regions of earth and water. Polish astronomer Nicolaus Copernicus was the first to make the successful case for our planet as a unified spherical body, which was to be represented not as a single connected landmass apart from water, but as a solid geological expanse whose chasms were filled with seas and oceans.

Linked to his revolutionary heliocentric model, Copernicus's global vision of world-space required an inversion of the conventional geocentric gaze extending from Earth outward to the cosmos. Henceforth, the modern conception of the global entailed the placing of an abstract point in outer space from which to look down or back onto our planet. Although Copernicus's global imaginary preceded the emergence of the modern international

Introduction / 11

system in the seventeenth century, it proved crucial for European geopolitics and imperialist expansionism. Most importantly, it enabled novel practices of geometrical and cultural demarcation: the carving up of world-space into "civilized" European sovereign states and "primitive" areas to be conquered and colonized. In other words, the abstract global world-space constructed by European astronomers and cartographers gave birth to a political world-space defined and shaped by relentless European strategies of global domination and resource extraction.

It took more than four centuries for Copernicus's global abstractions to assume an accessible pictorial form in the stunning images of *Earthrise*. Snapped in 1968 by Apollo 8 astronaut William Anders during the first-ever manned orbit of the moon, these photos reveal the haunting fragility of our tiny blue-white marble suspended in the vast expanse of the universe. Reaching a global audience almost instantaneously, the photos did much to enhance people's awareness of their collective journey on Spaceship Earth. For the first time in history, people blessed with access to televisions or illustrated magazines could see their home planet through the eyes of the Greek god Apollo, whose name adorned the U.S. space mission.[13]

These extraordinary images of our *global village* also demonstrated the crucial role of visuality and emotions in stimulating human imagination of the world as a whole.[14] Ideas and sentiments of belonging were now expanded and mediated through planetary images. The significance of planetary visuality was reinforced by new ecological perspectives such as the influential GAIA model. A British scientist working for NASA, James Lovelock, presented this catching theory of Earth as a single superorganism that functioned as a self-regulating global system. Such holistic perspectives contributed to the forging of transnational environmental movements in the 1960s and 1970s. Images of Planet Earth suddenly appeared on T-shirts, tote bags, coffee mugs, and counterculture magazines like the popular *Whole Earth Catalogue*. Unsurprisingly, it was during these opening decades of the space age that the use of *global* in popular and academic discourse skyrocketed.

Today, most globalization theorists consider *global* as something more encompassing than what is signified by the related words *transnational* or *international*. As we discuss throughout the book, a growing number of thinkers have settled on the terms *glocal* and *glocalization* to indicate the mutual interpretation of local and global spatial scales: the global manifests in local places just as the local is projected onto the global level. Ultimately, what makes a process or issue global or glocal has little to do with the trendy practice of dropping the adjective in front of a growing number of nouns. Rather, the global comes to life in the sort of questions we ask about the planetary dimensions of our existence that play themselves out in concrete events and dynamics across all spatial scales running from the local and the national to the global.[15]

We can now reconnect the two grammatical components of our keyword—*global* and *ization*—to arrive at a basic definition of globalization as a *set of processes involving the expansion and intensification of social relations and consciousness across world-space and world-time.* Still, we need to consider some important qualifications. First, globalization is a geographically uneven set of processes involving people, ideas, institutions, and objects. It does not happen everywhere at the same time, in the same way, or with the same intensity. Second, as noted above, multiple spatial scales intersect as the global shapes the local and vice-versa. Third, globalization does not always manifest as intensifying worldwide social relations and consciousness. Disjointed move-

Introduction / 13

ments among the distinct globalization processes can inhibit flows and disable existing links.

Moving on to our next core concept, let us note that globalization presupposes the existence of an evolving condition of *globality*. In other words, globalization produces globality as a possible outcome. Containing both spatial and social meanings, globality has been cast by some thinkers we discuss in chapter 3 as a *social condition* reflected in *supraterritoriality*: the gradual construction of a single social space on a global scale. Supraterritoriality is reflected in the emergence of large spatial dynamics that are relatively delinked from national territory, such as the Internet or global commodity chains.[16] At the same time, globalization theorists recognize that globality constitutes a rather fluid condition comprised of specific worldwide relations that can ebb as they did during the interwar period. Narratives of globality as a social condition often reflect northern viewpoints. As we shall see, some of these observers equate globality with a new phase of Western modernity. Dissenters, however, argue for a rupture between the social conditions of European modernity and globality that marks the beginning of a global age.[17]

Other globalization theorists define globality as a *form of consciousness* of the world as a single place.[18] Their focus on subjectivity implies a growing awareness of globality being assembled through intercultural exchanges and worldwide cultural flows. It also invites the observation that people's enhanced reflection on global processes is, in itself, a major component of the planetary totality of human relations.

Still other thinkers equate globality with a *system* or *network*. Some are influenced by Marxist analysis and hence describe the systemic structure of globality as a qualitatively new form of global capitalism. As place-based capital has become increasingly transnational through practices of *outsourcing* and *offshoring*, the production system as a whole is said to have moved from a "world economy" anchored in national circuits of accumulation to a "global economy" controlled by a transnational capitalist class supported by a transnational state.[19] Other globalization theorists reject a narrow economic approach and consider globality as a consequence of broader political and cultural processes. These include the globalization of institutional norms and standards and the worldwide distribution of cultural resources.[20]

To be sure, there exists significant conceptual overlap among these three meanings of globality. For example, a perspective on globality as an evolving social condition of worldwide interconnectivity can easily be complemented by an understanding of globality as consciousness of the world as a single place. At the same time, globality can be pictured as a worldwide system of transplanetary connectivity in which various elements interact with each other in complex ways. Over time, processes of globalization establish specific patterns of globality that invite new empirical inquiries.

On the surface, globality conjures up a *cosmopolitan world* in which dense interconnectivities of all sorts have significantly weakened or even dismantled national spaces. However, this idealized image of *one world* changes when linked to the realities of our twenty-first-century world in which nation-states are still capable of setting definite limits to the depth and breadth of globalization processes.[21] Hence, globality should be understood as an evolving condition resembling a messy construction site rather than a brand-new apartment building.

Like all social conditions, globality also extends to the subjective level expressed in individual narratives that contain normative judgments about whether globalization should be considered a good or bad thing. Our final core concept, *globalism*, highlights the crucial role of *ideology*, which has been an increasingly popular research subject of globalization theorists.[22] Ideologies are widely shared systems of ideas and beliefs that are accepted as truth by significant groups in society and legitimize particular power interests. They offer people a more or less coherent picture of the world not only as it is, but also how it ought to be. Ideologies organize the complexity of human experiences into simple mental maps that serve as guide and compass for social and political action. At the same time, dominant ideologies prompt the construction of counterideologies that challenge prevailing ideas and claims.

Globalization processes have exerted a transformative impact on the ideological landscape of the last century. These changes are reflected in the proliferation of the prefix *neo-* that has become attached to such conventional ideologies as *liberalism*, *conservatism*, and *fascism*. The novelty of these *neo-isms* lies in their ability to articulate the evolving global imaginary in concrete political programs and agendas. Three major variants of globalism arose at the turn of the twenty-first century and have competed with each other for the allegiance of a worldwide audience: *market globalism*, *justice globalism*, and *religious globalism*.

Market globalism emerged in the 1980s as the dominant political ideology extolling the virtues of globally integrating markets and free trade. Its codification and public dissemination fell largely to *neoliberal power elites* residing predominantly in the Global North. *Neoliberalism* is a rather broad concept built upon the classical liberal ideals of the self-regulating market and minimal state interference in the economy. Although it comes in several variations, neoliberalism is based on the free-market vision of the Nobel Prize–winning economist Milton Friedman,

U.S. president Ronald Reagan, and British prime minister Margaret Thatcher. These prominent economists and politicians built their neoliberal policy on the deregulation of national economies, the privatization of state-owned enterprises, the liberalization of trade, and massive income- and corporate tax cuts.

By the end of the 1990s, market globalists found themselves challenged by a growing global justice movement. Its members articulated the rising global imaginary by emphasizing the values of equality, global social justice, diversity, democracy, nonviolence, solidarity, ecological sustainability, and planetary citizenship. The ideological codification of justice globalism happened in important alternative spaces such as the World Social Forum based in the Global South. At the annual gathering of the thousands of organizations that made up the global justice movement, the leading voices of the World Social Forum criticized market globalism and its neoliberal program as the force behind increasing social inequalities, environmental destruction, and the further disempowerment of marginalized people around the world.

In addition, market globalism was challenged in the 1990s and 2000s by the forces of religious globalism. Al-Qaeda and ISIS represent two prominent Islamist organizations that articulate the rising global imaginary in apocalyptic terms. Other visions of a single global community united by religious faith have been assembled by groups such as the Army of God, Christian Identity, the Mormon Church, Falun Gong, Aum Shinrikyo, and Chabad, an orthodox Jewish movement with global ambitions. The ideological codifiers of religious globalism reject modern secularism and insist on the subordination of politics to faith. Crucially, Jihadist Islamists employ core concepts of *umma*—the

Introduction / 17

global community of believers—and *jihad*—global struggle against unbelief—to articulate their political program of global hegemony. To be sure, religious globalism in the form of Islamist jihadism still retains potent metaphors that resonate with people's national or even tribal solidarities. But its violent vision represents an ideological alternative to both market globalism and justice globalism that imagines community in unambiguously global terms.

During the 2010s, national populists around the world made *globalism* and *globalization* pejorative terms and linked them to allegedly elite-engineered efforts of weakening national communities. By the end of the decade, many of these antiglobalist movements had scored major victories at the ballot box that propelled their leaders into positions of power. Their political success demonstrated the ability of antiglobalist populism to adapt to multiple national and cultural environments such as Donald Trump's United States, Jair Bolsonaro's Brazil, Rodrigo Duterte's Philippines, and Viktor Orbán's Hungary. Their denouncement of globalism notwithstanding, national populists and their ideas amount to a global phenomenon. For this reason, a growing number of globalization theorists have focused their recent research efforts on the twenty-first-century ideological struggle between globalisms and several variants of national populism.[23]

To sum up, the core concepts of globalization theory covered in this section refer to globally interconnected processes, conditions, imaginaries, and ideologies. As discussed in the ensuing chapters, the failure of some thinkers to clearly delineate their core concepts has provoked critics to question the value of globalization theory in general. Hence, globalization theory requires precise definitions to demarcate distinct aspects of the worldwide compression of space and time.

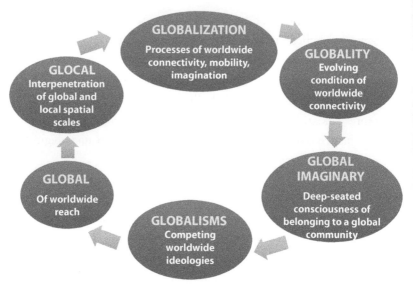

Figure 3. Core concepts of globalization theory

Qualitative Attributes

Globalization is theorized mostly along three qualitative attributes or properties: *(inter)connectivity*, *mobility*, and *imagination*. Connectivity refers to the forging of human relations that are the prerequisite for all social action. Social relations can range from the intimate connections among family members and friends to expanded communal relations such as those involving economic systems of production and exchange and networks of scientific inquiry. Global interconnectivity names a social quality created by processes of worldwide expansion and acceleration of social relations.

As we noted before, people tend to experience growing global connections as multiplication of contacts and shrinkage of distance. This spatial compression, in turn, enhances their sense of *transworld simultaneity*—connections extended across world-space at the same time—and *transworld instantaneity*—worldwide connections forged in no time.[24] Consider the explosion of 24/7 digital networks of interconnectivity in the twenty-first century. The effortlessness and ubiquity of contacts established and maintained via social media sites like Meta or YouTube has been one of the most celebrated globalization stories in public discourse.

Big Tech corporations like Amazon, Google, and Netflix rely on complex digital platforms and decentralized production hubs to create and distribute their products and services worldwide. 5G technology, Artificial Intelligence (AI), machine learning, and the Internet of Things (IoT) facilitate the extension of digital social relations with connections among proliferating electronic devices. In 2024, the IoT connected more than seventeen billion devices. This number is projected to reach trillions by 2040.[25] Thickening circuits of digital connectivity add new layers of technological complexity, which require higher levels of *synchronization* of social interactions. As will be discussed in chapter 3, globalization theories focused on growing social and technological complexity have taken up increasing space in the pertinent literature.

Multiplying global connections, digital or otherwise, often translates into new efficiencies, conveniences, and general enhancement of living standards. But the forging of connections functions on a logic of inclusion and exclusion. This means that networks do not necessarily empower all people. In fact, the technological hyperconnectivity underpinning globalizing markets has failed to close the inequality gap between the privileged Global North and the disadvantaged South. The exacerbation of global inequity has serious social consequences. As global connectivity fails to deliver for the vast majority of people on this planet, extremist ideologies can fuel angry social movements. The globalization backlash behind the recent surge of national populism is a stark reminder of the inadequacy of global connections without social justice.

As noted above, theorizing globalization in terms of growing connections also extends to matters of consciousness. The global circulation of ideas, ideologies, imaginaries, images, narratives, metaphors, myths, and symbols is just as important as the proliferation of material linkages. Recall how imaginings of the world as a single place were greatly stimulated by the Apollo pictures of Earthrise. Plotting globalization on this second qualitative property—*imagination*—requires a closer examination of the significance of expanding *social imaginaries*. These deep-seated background understandings provide the general parameters within which people imagine their communal belonging. The *national imaginary* of earlier centuries centered on notions and feelings of belonging to the nation-state. Over the past decades, the intensifying experience of growing interconnectivity has strengthened imaginations of community in global terms. As we noted previously, this rising *global imaginary* sets the general parameters of how people fit together across political borders and how they should interact with each other.[26] It provides people in concrete local settings with shared global standards showing how to structure their everyday lives and social routines.

The third qualitative attribute of globalization, *mobility*, facilitates concepts like flows, networks, and movements. Apart from human migration studies, spatial mobility has been poorly theorized in the social sciences. Globalization thinkers have been at the forefront of a recent "mobility turn."[27] As we discuss in the ensuing chapters, globalization theory is replete with metaphors for spatial and temporal movements such as *deterritorialization, supraterritoriality, global village, scapes, time-space compression, distanci-*

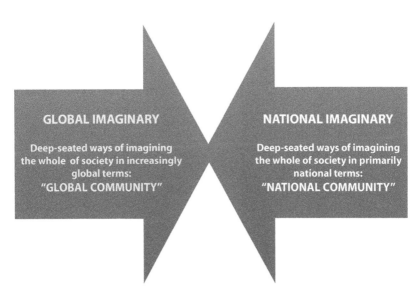

Figure 4. Social imaginaries

ation, network society, space of flows, timeless time, global fluids, and so on. Dynamics of spatial movement pertain to human bodies crisscrossing the globe as tourists, refugees, migrants, retirees, international students, businesspeople, backpackers, and guest workers. But they also include the transplanetary flows of animals, plants, bacteria, viruses, tradable commodities, industrial waste, capital, corporations, organizations, ideas, images, data, and so on. With the rise of electronic modes of mobility, daily trips between physical space and virtual space have become routine for people on the privileged side of the digital divide. Indeed, our planet itself manifests as a *terra mobilis*. Its crust, mantle, and core are in perpetual motion and constantly reshape the biosphere. The concepts *Anthropocene* and *ecocide* examined below capture the reverse movement of people and objects impacting the materiality of our planet by accelerating climate change and reducing biodiversity.

22 / *Introduction*

The mapping of globalization processes on these three qualitative properties deepens the sophistication of theoretical research on the subject. At the same time, however, we must bear in mind that connections, imaginations, and mobilities intersect and overlap in the social world in complex ways.

Quantitative Measurements

Regardless of whether globalization thinkers select scientific, interpretive, or emancipatory ways of theorizing, they cannot afford to ignore hard data about people, objects, ideas, and institutions crossing national borders. Empirically informed assessments of the causes, contents, and consequences of globalization are crucial not only for theory formation and development, but also for tackling concrete policy issues such as trade or education. Over the last three decades, efforts have been underway to provide useful quantitative measurements of globalization in the form of indexes.

An *index* is an indicator, or measure, that provides empirical information about a phenomenon. Major globalization indexes include the A. T. Kearney / Foreign Policy Globalization Index, the KOF Index of Globalization, and the DHL Global Connectedness Index. There have even been recent attempts to develop a Global Consciousness Index, which would measure people's awareness and meanings of the world as a single place.[28] Let us take a closer look at the latter to better understand how, exactly, globalization indexes measure the worldwide compression of space and time.

The DHL Global Connectedness Index, for example, gauges the depth and breadth of a country's integration with the rest of the world, as manifested by its participation in transnational

Introduction / 23

flows of products and services (trade flows), capital (investment flows), information (electronic data flows), and people (tourism, student, and migrant flows). *Depth* refers to the size of international flows as compared to a relevant measure of the size of all interactions of that type, both transnational and domestic. It reflects how important or pervasive interactions across national borders are in the context of business or life. *Breadth* measures how closely each country's distribution of international flows across its partner countries matches the global distribution of the same flows in the opposite direction. The breadth of a country's merchandise exports, for example, is measured based on the difference between the distribution of its exports across destination countries versus the rest of the world's distribution of merchandise imports. These country-level results are aggregated using the overall flows as weights to determine the worldwide level of breadth.

The DHL Global Connectedness Index is built primarily from internationally comparable data from multicountry sources, with additional data drawn from national statistics. Worldwide depth ratios are calculated using published estimates for the world, rather than being aggregated from individual countries' reported data. Worldwide breadth estimates are calculated using reporting country data on interactions with all partners. In cases where adequate data are not available from a reporting country but sufficient coverage can be achieved by using flows in the opposite direction as reported by partners, this method is used to calculate breadth. Finally, overall depth and breadth scores are computed using sophisticated weighting schemes.[29]

Although most globalization indexes combine cultural, economic, ecological, political, and social elements of globalization, the measurement outcomes can vary immensely as a result of

24 / *Introduction*

the dimensions included and relative weight assigned to those aspects.[30] A number of globalization theorists have argued that quantitative measurements of globalization have too many weaknesses. Problems concern the lack of commonly agreed on theoretical definitions, the difficulties of operationalizing dynamics on multiple spatial levels, an outdated focus on nation-states, and access to suitable large data sets. Hence, many globalization scholars rely on a "mixed-methods" approach based on the integration of quantitative and qualitative analyses.

A VERY BRIEF HISTORY OF GLOBALIZATION THEORY

Although we will engage relevant historical matters in more detail in the following chapters, it is necessary to round out our preliminary inventory of the nuts and bolts of globalization theory with a brief account of relevant developments. When and where did globalization theory emerge and how did it evolve?

It was Euro-American social theory, particularly in the form of macro theories of social change, that stimulated the initial turn to globalization in the late 1980s and early 1990s. Social theory is embedded within the larger academic discipline of sociology, which is dedicated to the development of systematic knowledge about social life. But the roots of modern social theory lie in knowledge systems that were designed and shaped in the Global North at the height of nineteenth-century European and U.S. imperialism. Hence, it is not surprising that leading social theorists neglected to account for their field's long and multiple origins reaching back centuries and including thinkers located on all continents.

Ibn Khaldūn, for example, was a fourteenth-century North African diplomat and scholar who pioneered the scientific study of society. He created the transdisciplinary field of *'ilm-al'umran* (science of culture), which covered the modern disciplines of history, sociology, economics, and anthropology. Employing comparative case studies in his search for causal social relationships, Ibn Khaldūn developed a large body of empirical work on state formation and the sources of social solidarity. His masterpiece, *al-Muqaddima* ("Introduction"), constitutes an original treatise on social cohesion in societies of the Maghreb region (Northwestern Africa). The book treats a central theme in Émile Durkheim's French school of structural functionalism founded nearly five hundred years later. Ibn Khaldūn's sophisticated analysis of historical cycles of social change strongly contrasts with the linear and progressive theories of social development favored by modern European thinkers.[31] Still, most contemporary sociology textbooks pass over the field's non-Western origins in almost complete silence, dating the emergence of *classical social theory* in nineteenth-century Europe.

Hence, it is imperative that we acknowledge from the start of this book the impact of Eurocentrism in the formation of social theory, which has also been casting a lingering shadow on globalization theory. After all, social inquiry and its methods produce new ideas and institutions. They do not simply describe the world as it is, but also *make* concrete social realities.[32] One of the principal shapers of the modern globalizing world was the European version of social theory. A product of the Enlightenment, the rise of science, the formation of modern states, the ascent of industrial capitalism, and northern imperialist practices, it became the authoritative paradigm centered on social dynamics linked to worldwide extension and intensification of Western modernity. Classical social thinkers—especially Karl Marx, Max Weber, Émile Durkheim, and Georg Simmel—

developed immensely influential theories that made rationality, capitalism, industrialism, the division of labor, and bureaucratization the driving forces of social change.

On the upside, these privileged texts did contain some global perspectives, such as Marx's writings on British colonialism in India and Weber and Durkheim's comparative sociologies of religion. On the downside, these theories were built on the Eurocentric assumption of a vast global difference separating advanced Western societies from the lagging "rest" of the world, much of which was under direct European colonial rule. Herbert Spencer's evolutionary theory of *social Darwinism* represents one of the most extreme examples of the Eurocentric claim of global difference that facilitated the spread of biological determinism and white supremacy in the first half of the twentieth century.

This taken-for-granted superiority of Western society lived on in a less invidious form in post–World War II modernization theories, which envisioned economic development in linear stages moving from "lower" traditional societies to "higher" modern industrial societies. Modernization was presented as a universal paradigm that societies in the Global South were wise to adapt. Thus, the Northern-led industrial development of the Global South was legitimized as a "progressive" project that would help these "underdeveloped" regions catch up with their mature tutors.[33]

This long intellectual legacy of theorizing social change in the context of an imagined beneficial worldwide expansion of European modernity influenced the new globalization talk that emerged in the 1980s and 1990s. At the same time, some of the pioneering social theorists who served as the midwives of globalization theory had been exposed to more recent revisionist frameworks rooted in Marxist perspectives that focused on worldwide patterns of inequality rooted in long-standing relationships between the Global North and Global South.

One of the most significant of these precursors of globalization theory was *world-systems theory*, which served as a generic label for various explanations of large-scale social change originating in sixteenth-century Europe. The proponents of this approach adopted as their basic unit of analysis a single world-system rooted in structural components of the world economy.[34] They argued that the *modern world-system* was driven by the exploitative logic of capital accumulation. It had combined with nineteenth-century imperialist Western practices to produce unequal regions in the world-system. The rich *core* was situated in Europe and North America and exploited the *periphery* in the Global South for labor and raw materials. Positioned between the core and periphery, the developing *semiperiphery* shared characteristics of both. Thus, world-systems theory presented hegemonic states in the Global North as the key drivers of the modern world economy of capitalism. Their principal function was to coordinate and reproduce the asymmetrical power relations that preserved the economic superiority of the core.

The dominant historical account of the evolution of globalization theory acknowledges the early impact of world-systems theory. At the same time, the conventional narrative explains the formation of a distinct theoretical globalization framework as a development in three *stages* or *waves* that followed each other in quick succession.[35] These waves were said to correspond to three competing camps of globalization thinkers referred to as *hyperglobalizers*, *skeptics*, and *transformationalists*.[36] Each theoretical current is alleged to have generated distinct arguments and models of globalization that put them at odds with each other.

According to this conventional historical account, the relatively small, but influential, group of *hyperglobalizers* made up the bulk of the first wave of globalization theory in the early 1990s. They considered globalization as the primary driver of most contemporary social change and emphasized an epochal shift in the interconnectedness of societies from the modern age to the global era. Employing sweeping economistic narratives, these first-wave thinkers predicted an eventual "denationalization" of economies through the expansion of transnational networks of production, trade, and finance. Hyperglobalizers include thinkers who celebrated new forms of digital connectivity as the indispensable central nervous system of the coming "borderless world."[37] The growing power of digital capitalism was alleged to go hand in hand with the weakening of nationalist sentiments that sat at the core of crucial modern legal notions such as state sovereignty and territorial integrity.

The first wave of hyperglobalist globalization theory is said to have lost much of its momentum by the turn of the twenty-first century. Two successive waves materialized quickly. Committed to less polemical and more empirically oriented globalization theories, *skeptics* emphasize the continuing significance of nation-states and regional dynamics. These critics often charge the hyperglobalist camp with overemphasizing the role of historical rupture, which led to the exaggeration of the decline of the nation-state and the associated failure to appreciate the enduring significance of the post–World War II international system. Moreover, second-wave skeptics insist that today's expanding social networks do not contain a singular, worldwide principle of interaction or integration. For them, globalization represents just another phase of capitalist modernization in the form of limited regional economic networks led by prosperous countries in North America, Europe, Asia, and Oceania.[38]

The third wave corresponds to the camp of *transformationalists*, who consider globalization a powerful deterritorializing set of processes moving societies toward increasing global interconnectivity and mobility. Unlike hyperglobalists, however, transformationalists hold more moderate expectations about the pace, breadth, and depth of social change. Moreover, they resist the hyperglobalist reduction of globalization to economics of the free-market capitalist variety. Instead, they divide their research attention among what they consider three equally important dimensions of globalization: economics, politics, and culture. Finally, the transformationalist camp is said to sympathize with the skeptical insight that "globalization" can sometimes be a misnomer for smaller regional and national dynamics.[39]

To its credit, this conventional *three waves and three camps model* provided a first historical narrative of theoretical perspectives that emerged and developed in the last three decades. It served as a useful initial typology for organizing ideas about globalization. But there are also some serious problems with this conventional framework. First, it draws overly sharp boundaries around each wave and camp. As our discussion in this book will show, overlaps among various currents of globalization theory have been quite common. Historical and analytical schemes that tend to minimize these interactions often miss out on important common ground. Second, the representation of globalization theories as following each other in neat linear waves is belied by the real-world messiness of simultaneous engagements and cross-currents. For example, some skeptical accounts actually emerged around the same time as hyperglobalist narratives.

30 / *Introduction*

Similarly, some of the earliest globalization theorists could be classified as "transformationalists." Finally, the theories developed by leading thinkers were often much richer and more varied than those linked to the rather reductionistic categories of hyperglobalizers, skeptics, and transformationalists.

PLAN OF THE BOOK

Given these enduring shortcomings of the conventional historical narrative and analytical framework of globalization theory, this book is based on a different conceptual structure. It organizes globalization theories by connecting four analytically distinct *modes of theorizing*—or styles of thinking about globalization—to their corresponding outcomes: *general theories, domain theories, complexity theories,* and *critical theories.*[40] While this novel *modality framework* recognizes the existence of real differences among these categories, it also identifies important synergies and intersections that have stimulated innovative insights.

Accordingly, each chapter in this book introduces a specific theoretical category such as complexity theory—and the form of thinking that produced it (complexity mode of theorizing)—with reference to the corresponding ideas and frameworks of exemplary globalization theorists. But rather than overwhelming readers with a flurry of names and arguments, the number of spotlighted thinkers will be limited to influential figures who set the conceptual stage for enduring globalization debates. We need to remember that the purpose of this book is to meet the three basic challenges identified in the preface: to provide a *concise overview* of important globalization theories; to present these difficult materials in a *clearly organized manner,* using *acces-*

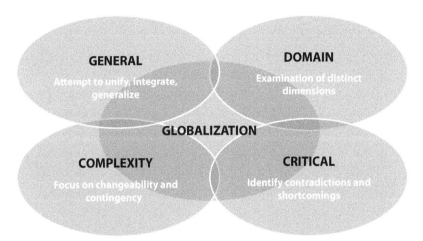

Figure 5. Modes of theorizing globalization

sible language while maintaining intellectual sophistication; and to *sharpen our ability to make normative judgments*.

The key thinkers and their styles of inquiry covered in this book have proven themselves to be perfectly capable of reaching across several modalities. Yet, they have also shown a special affinity for one particular way of thinking. Their mastery of this chosen mode shaped the selection of key themes, the methodologies they employed, and the presentation of their findings. In short, *their forms of theorizing and their resulting theories are linked and should be presented as such*. The modality framework of the book will make it easier for readers to discover their own affinity for certain globalization theories—and their corresponding styles of thinking—and thus inspire them to plant their own conceptual flag in the sprawling intellectual terrain.

The *general theories* examined in chapter 1 are the result of macro-level inquiries into globalization processes. They relate to and incorporate traditional themes of social theory such as modernization, industrialization, the division of labor, social stratification, secularization, stages of social and economic development, and capitalism. Thus, theorists tend to construct their globalization models in the generalizing or *grand theory* style of classical social thinkers such as Karl Marx, Max Weber, and Émile Durkheim. The chapter covers pioneering frameworks for a historical periodization of globalization as well as influential analyses of the relationship between globalization and modernity. Our discussion ends with a close consideration of holistic mappings of multidimensional globalization processes.

The *domain theories* examined in chapter 2 are produced by thinkers who prefer to explore significant globalization dynamics that correspond to their own area of academic expertise while at the same time utilizing the insights of transdisciplinary scholarship. The chapter focuses on key theories covering three major dimensions of globalization: economics, politics, and culture. Our survey includes innovative ways of analyzing global capitalism as well as insightful evaluations of globalization as a force shaping new forms of territoriality and sovereignty. Our consideration of opposing theories of clashing cultural differences and intensifying cultural sameness is rounded out by perspectives that interpret cultural globalization as a process of hybridization.

The *complexity theories* explored in chapter 3 are the outcome of a style of thinking that approaches globalization as a changeable and highly contingent set of social dynamics. Thus, complexity theorists enjoy close encounters with multiple layers of social networks, systems, and interdependencies. They also favor the design of cutting-edge transdisciplinary research tools and methodologies that illuminate the rich and intricate patterns of global social change across the full range of social analysis extending from the micro level to the macro level. Introducing thinkers who explore the shifting spatial arrangements created by globalization, this chapter also considers theorists who apply the complexity mode to envision a "global network society" suspended in intricate webs of digital information and communication.

The *critical theories* discussed in chapter 4 include wholesale denunciations of existing globalization theories as well as more sympathetic and constructive criticisms that address various concerns. One influential mode of critical thinking decries the "folly" of circular reasoning, which manifests in the practice of globalization theorists to make globalization both the cause and effect of social change. In other words, critics charge that globalization presented as an outcome cannot be explained by also invoking globalization as a cause producing this outcome. Other critics draw on postcolonial theory to call for the greater inclusion of Global South perspectives articulated by marginalized thinkers who still find themselves on the short end of the stick of Western modernity and its violent legacy of imperialism and colonialism. Still other critical thinkers demand closer attention to the persistence and, in some cases, the escalation of different forms of social injustices around the world.

Given that the bulk of the thinkers introduced and discussed in the previous chapters were globalization pioneers writing mostly in the 1990s and early 2000s, chapter 5 examines important *new theories* that have emerged in more recent years. The new generation of globalization thinkers presented in this chapter have become more self-reflective and attuned to the rapidly shifting dynamics of worldwide interconnectivity and mobility in our unsettled and volatile times. The chapter highlights

34 / *Introduction*

current theoretical debates over deglobalization, the advancing digitization of global interactions, and the rapidly changing ecological conditions of life on our planet.

In the spirit of constructive criticism, each chapter concludes with a balanced evaluation of major strengths and weaknesses of the discussed mode of theorizing globalization. An appended Brief Guide to Further Readings at the end of the book offers useful bibliographic information to readers who wish to expand their exposure to globalization theories.

NOTES

1. Richard Swedberg, *The Art of Social Theory* (Princeton, NJ: Princeton University Press, 2015), 236.

2. Max Horkheimer, "Traditional and Critical Theory," in Max Horkheimer, *Critical Theory: Selected Essays* (New York: Herder & Herder, 1972), 188–243.

3. Thomas Kuhn, *The Structure of Scientific Revolutions*, 2nd ed. (Chicago: University of Chicago Press, 1970), 10–11.

4. Craig Calhoun, "Introduction," in Craig Calhoun, Joseph Gerteis, James Moody, Steven Pfaff, and Indermohan Virk, eds., *Classical Sociological Theory*, 3rd ed. (Chichester, UK; Wiley-Blackwell, 2012), 3.

5. Swedberg, *Art of Social Theory*, 6.

6. Joep Cornelissen, Markus A. Höllerer, and David Seidl, "What Theory Is and Can Be: Forms of Theorizing in Organizational Scholarship," *Organizational Theory* 2 (2021): 6.

7. Jan Nederveen Pieterse, *Connectivity and Global Studies* (Cham, Switzerland: Palgrave Macmillan, 2021), 55.

8. Manfred B. Steger, *The Rise of the Global Imaginary: Political Ideologies from the French Revolution to the Global War on Terror* (Oxford, UK: Oxford University Press, 2008).

9. Manfred B. Steger and Amentahru Wahlrab, *What Is Global Studies? Theory and Practice* (London: Routledge, 2017).

10. Eve Darian-Smith and Philip C. McCarty, *The Global Turn: Theories, Research Designs, and Methods for Global Studies* (Oakland: University of California Press, 2017), 2.

11. For a detailed genealogical discussion of the concept *globalization* and the evolution of its meaning, see Manfred B. Steger and Paul James, eds, *Globalization: The Career of a Concept* (London: Routledge, 2015).

12. Raymond Williams, *Keywords: A Vocabulary of Culture and Society* (Oxford, UK: Oxford University Press, 2014).

13. Denis Cosgrove, *Apollo's Eye: A Cartographic Genealogy of the Earth in the Western Imagination* (Baltimore: Johns Hopkins University Press, 2001); Benjamin Lazier, "Earthrise; or, The Globalization of the World Picture," *American Historical Review* 116, no. 3 (2011): 602–30.

14. Tommaso Durante, "International Relations, New Global Studies, and the Epistemic Power of the Image," *New Global Studies* (2020), https://doi.org/10.1515/ngs-2020-0038; Deirdre McKay, "Affect: Making the Global through Care," in Hilary E. Kahn, ed., *Framing the Global: Entry Points for Research* (Bloomington: Indiana University Press, 2014), 18–36.

15. Darian-Smith and McCarty, *Global Turn*, 3–4.

16. Jan Aart Scholte, *Globalization: A Critical Introduction*, 2nd ed. (Houndmills, UK: Palgrave Macmillan, 2005), 60–61.

17. See, for example, Anthony Giddens, *The Consequences of Modernity* (Stanford, CA: Stanford University Press, 1990); and Martin Albrow, *The Global Age* (Stanford, CA: Stanford University Press, 1997).

18. Roland Robertson, *Globalization: Social Theory and Global Culture* (London: Sage, 1992).

19. William Robinson, *A Theory of Global Capitalism* (Baltimore: Johns Hopkins University Press, 2004).

20. Barrie Axford, *Theories of Globalization* (Cambridge, UK: Polity, 2013); David Singh Grewal, *Network Power: The Social Dynamics of Globalization* (New Haven, CT: Yale University Press, 2008).

21. Pankaj Ghemawat, *The Laws of Globalization and Business Applications* (Cambridge, UK: Cambridge University Press, 2017).

22. Manfred B. Steger, *Globalisms: Facing the Populist Challenge* (Lanham, MD: Rowman & Littlefield, 2020); Rafal Soborski, *Ideology in a Global Age* (Houndmills, UK: Palgrave Macmillan, 2013); Pieter de

36 / *Introduction*

Wilde, "The Making of Four Ideologies of Globalization," *European Political Science Review* 11, no. 1 (2018): 1–18.

23. See, for example, Barrie Axford, *Populism vs the New Globalization* (London: Sage, 2021).

24. Pieterse, *Connectivity and Global Studies*, 29; Scholte, *Globalization*, 61.

25. National Intelligence Council, *Global Trends 2040: A More Contested World* (March 2021), 3; www.dni.gov/nic/globaltrends.

26. Charles Taylor, *Modern Social Imaginaries* (Durham. NC: Duke University Press, 2004), 23–26; Steger, *Rise of the Global Imaginary*.

27. John Urry, *Mobilities* (Cambridge, UK: Polity, 2007); Aharon Kellerman, *Globalization and Spatial Mobilities: Commodities and People, Capital, Information and Technology* (Cheltenham, UK; Edward Elgar Publishing, 2020); Noel B. Salazar, "Key Figures of Mobility: An Introduction," *Social Anthropology* 25, no. 1 (2017): 5–12.

28. Thomas Stieve, "The Wikipedia Global Consciousness Index: A Measurement of Awareness and Meaning of the World as a Single Place," *Globalizations* 19, no. 1 (2021): 118–38, http://doi.org/10.1080/147477 31.2020.1857628.

29. Stephen A. Altman and Caroline R. Bastion, *DHL Global Connectedness Index 2021 Update*, www.dhl.com/content/dam/dhl/global/dhl-spotlight/documents/pdf/2021-gci-update-report.pdf, 54–56.

30. Pim Martens, Marco Caselli, Philippe De Lombaerde, Lukas Figge, and Jan Aart Scholte, "New Directions in Globalization Indices," *Globalizations* 12, no. 4 (2015): 222.

31. George Ritzer and Jeffrey Stepinsky, *Classical Sociological Theory*, 7th ed. (London: Sage, 2018), 8.

32. John Law and John Urry, "Enacting the Social," *Economy and Society* 33, no. 3 (2004): 390–410.

33. W. W. Rostow, *The Stages of Economic Growth: A Non-Communist Manifesto* (Cambridge, UK: Cambridge University Press, 1960).

34. See, for example, Immanuel Wallerstein, *The Capitalist World Economy* (Cambridge, UK: Cambridge University Press, 1979); Wallerstein, *World-Systems Analysis: An Introduction* (Durham, NC: Duke University Press, 2004); Christopher Chase-Dunn, *Global Formation: Structures of the World Economy* (Lanham, MD: Rowman & Littlefield, 1998).

35. See, for example, David Held, Anthony McGrew, David Goldblatt, and Jonathan Perraton, eds., *Global Transformations* (Cambridge, UK: Polity Press, 1999); Colin Hay and David Marsh, eds., *Demystifying Globalization* (Basingstoke, UK: Palgrave, 2000); Luke Martell, *The Sociology of Globalization*, 2nd ed. (Cambridge, UK: Polity Press, 2017).

36. Held et al., *Global Transformations.*

37. See, for example, Kenichi Ohmae, *The Borderless World: Power and Strategy in the Interlinked World Economy* (New York: Harper Business, 1990); Ohmae, *The End of the Nation-State: The Rise of Regional Economies* (New York: Free Press, 1995).

38. See, for example, Paul Hirst and Grahame Thompson, *Globalization in Question* (Cambridge, UK: Polity Press, 1996); and Michael Mann, "Has Globalization Ended the Rise of the Nation-State?," *Review of International Political Economy* 4, no. 3 (1997): 472–96.

39. Held et al., *Global Transformations*; Scholte, *Globalization.*

40. Anthony McGrew and Andrew Jones also offer useful mappings of globalization literature according to similar categories they call "modes of inquiry" and "forms of thinking." However, their perspectives remain deeply embedded in the conventional "waves framework" that also overplays the alleged camp mentality separating key globalization thinkers. See Anthony McGrew, "Globalization in Hard Times: Contention in the Academy and Beyond," in Georg Ritzer, ed., *The Blackwell Companion to Globalization* (Oxford, UK: Blackwell Publishing, 2007), 32; and Andrew Jones, *Globalization: Key Thinkers* (Cambridge, UK: Polity Press, 2010), 9–11.

CHAPTER ONE

General Theories

This chapter commences our concise overview and discussion of major globalization theories. Focusing on conceptual models produced by a generalizing style of inquiry, we start our intellectual journey with a brief explanation of *general theory*. Showing how this framework applies to theorizing globalization, the bulk of the chapter introduces general theories of globalization with reference to the works of three important thinkers who laid the foundation for the heated globalization debates in the 2000s.

We pay particular attention to their selection of themes that lend themselves to a general mode of theorizing. We begin our discussion with a consideration of Roland Robertson's pioneering attempt to provide a framework for a historical periodization of globalization. While his framework represented a significant breakthrough in globalization theory, it remained largely beholden to linear and Eurocentric modernization theories.

Next, we turn to Anthony Giddens's tremendously influential analysis of the relationship between globalization and modernity, which treats the former as an extension of rather

General Theories / 39

than a break with the latter. Challenging Giddens's perspective, Martin Albrow instead argues for the dawn of a new epoch in history—the "Global Age"—which involves the supplanting of modernity with globality. While these two thinkers hold diametrically opposed positions on globalization, their models converge in their narrow focus on Western modernity at the expense of more multicentered frameworks.

Finally, we explore David Held's holistic mapping of multidimensional globalization processes. Despite some remaining flaws in their comprehensive framework, Held and his collaborators should be credited with making the most successful attempt yet to present a systematic and integrated theory of globalization.

The prominent theorists discussed in this chapter not only share a common fondness for macro-level approaches to their subject, but also exhibit a strong penchant for building upon the insights of classical Western social thinkers. Although these thinkers rely primarily on the generalizing mode of theorizing, they also resort to other styles such as the complexity and critical mode. The chapter ends with a critical evaluation of some strengths and weaknesses of the generalizing approach to globalization.

THE GENERALIZING MODE OF THEORIZING

General theory refers to a conceptual framework that attempts a holistic explanation of social or natural phenomena. Unlike domain theory, which focuses on particular dynamics occurring in clearly demarcated dimensions of knowledge, general theories identify patterns at the macro level and seek to integrate related relationships and linkages that span the spectrum of natural or social phenomena. Constructed at the top level of generality, such theories nonetheless aim for internal consistency and coherence of their propositions. In short, general theories cover a large number of occurrences that reach across multiple dimensions and involve extended time frames. The ultimate goal of general theorizing is to produce conceptual frameworks capable of generating comprehensive claims to universal validity and applicability.

In the natural sciences, for example, Albert Einstein's pathbreaking *General Theory of Relativity* (1915) postulated the relativity of space and time across the entire universe. It asserted the central role of gravity as a natural force capable of bending space. The Nobel Prize–winning German physicist then proceeded to apply his pioneering insights to related phenomena and the universe as a whole. Although Einstein's relativity paradigm proved to be superior to Isaac Newton's much earlier mechanistic theory of universal gravitation, both models are examples of macro frameworks generated through a generalizing mode of inquiry.

Similarly, in the social sciences, John Maynard Keynes's *General Theory of Employment, Interest, and Money* (1936) offered a systematic framework of modern macroeconomics capable of integrating different aspects of his chosen subject such as the industrial production and distribution of goods and services. The British economist's innovative general model challenged the conventional wisdom of classical economics, which had stipulated that national economies would always automatically revert to a state of general equilibrium after periods of severe crisis like the Great Depression of the 1930s. Keynes's generalizing thinking thoroughly revised our understanding of the workings of the forces of supply and demand in a way that justified significant government interference in national economies.

General Theories / 41

Between 1945 and the 1970s, this interventionist framework—aptly named *Keynesianism*—replaced the laissez-faire market model as the dominant paradigm of modern macroeconomics.

Yet, there are also clear downsides to general theorizing, such as its tendency to sell biased and partial truth-claims as objective and universal knowledge. Another concerns its penchant for totalizing claims and conceptual singularity—as in *globalization, modernity,* or *industrialization.* But why should the real-world processes to which these constructs refer not be plural and diverse—as in *globalizations, modernities,* or *industrializations?* As Jan Nederveen Pieterse observes, the singular is often used to maintain dominant knowledge paradigms: "While the singular implies convergence, the plural suggests diversity. The singular view is centripetal; the plural is centrifugal and decentering."[1]

Perhaps one of the most serious problems of general theorizing concerns the *violence of abstraction.* Theory-building at all levels invariably involves the separation of ideas about things from these tangible objects themselves. This necessary mental disconnection also applies to empirically grounded theories focused on practical application. For example, statistical data about the number of deaths in a given society over a specified period of time only make sense if they are connected to abstract constructs such as *mortality rates* and *age cohorts.* By plotting the total numbers of specific deaths onto classification charts, researchers gain the demographic knowledge necessary for the development of social policies. While all modes and levels of theorizing are paved with countless instances of such mental separation, the violence of abstraction is far greater in general theories that operate at a high level of abstraction and are thus several degrees further removed from empirical processes. Still, the generalist's goal of recognizing and analyzing *comprehensive patterns* can only be reached through the creation of high-order theoretical constructs and typologies that nonexperts often perceive as arcane and disconnected from the real world.

Such frustration with the inherent propensity of general theory to create highly abstract constructs that might not relate easily to the immediate concerns of everyday life also reverberates across academia. For example, one of the most trenchant criticisms of general social theory came from the sociologist C. Wright Mills in the late 1950s. Having dedicated his scholarly career to the analysis of specific power relations in American society, he coined the pejorative term *grand theory* to refer to abstract general models. Mills's main target was a popular general model of social systems known as *structural functionalism.* He presented Talcott Parsons and other originators of this framework as prime examples of *grand theorists* obsessed with concepts at the expense of tackling pressing social problems. For Mills, such general attempts to force a large number of social phenomena and processes into a single overarching theoretical framework were not only intellectually dubious but also socially irresponsible.[2]

To be sure, some points of Mills's hard-hitting criticism of grand theory address obvious problems of general theory. At the same time, however, we should note that the deprecating use of *grand* unduly diverts attention from some of the term's far more positive connotations such as *awesome, noble,* and *sublime.* As we will discover in the ensuing sections of this chapter, there is often something quite dignified—and even courageous—in the ambitious efforts of grand theorists to develop general models and overarching paradigms. In the same vein, globalization thinkers employ a generalizing mode of theorizing to aim for nothing less than a comprehensive understanding of social change on the global scale. At times, their quest requires a flirtation with the complexity mode of theorizing globalization covered in chapter 3.

Most generalizing globalization theorists build their models on the classical repertoire of major Western social thinkers such as Karl Marx, Max Weber, and Émile Durkheim. Claiming that some of their pioneering insights have withstood the test of time, globalization generalists tend to connect their own intellectual efforts to key themes in classical social theory such as modernization, industrialization, capitalism, division of labor, solidarity, class and social stratification, revolution, religion, and secularization, and to historical stages of social development. But the flipside of this productive connection to the classical foundations of social thought is that generalizing globalization thinkers tend to integrate into their models the built-in Eurocentric standpoints and standards.

Finally, general theory recognizes the importance of situating their globalization models within macro-historical frameworks. As a result of these efforts, perhaps the most important foundational questions that animate general theorizing about globalization concern its *history* and relate to matters of *origins* and *periodization*: when did globalization start, and what is the best way of charting its historical development over time?

HISTORICIZING GLOBALIZATION

Many globalization pioneers writing at the turn of the twenty-first century responded to these crucial historical questions by emphasizing the relative novelty of the process, dating its origins back decades or, at most, two centuries. Although longer-term models emerged in globalization theory, generalizing thinkers have constructed several competing *analytical models* to

44 / General Theories

explain the origins of globalization.[3] The first perspective denies that globalization has *any* geographic or temporal origin. Instead, it argues that the *instinctual urge* to search for a better life in other regions of our planet is *hardwired* into human brains. This biological, and rather deterministic, explanation presents globalization as a perennial process that might one day be extended beyond the globe in the colonization of our solar system and even further parts of the universe.

The second analytical model rejects biological determinism in favor of a socially produced *long-term cyclical process*. This means that globalization is a social dynamic that has unfolded in periodic fits and starts that result in the eventual construction of new cycles. While each particular cycle has its own origin, globalization understood as an assemblage of successive cycles possesses multiple origins.

The third analytical framework proposes *specific dated events* that launched globalization some decades or centuries ago. Favorite candidates include the early 1990s (the information and communications technology or ICT revolution); 1989–91 (the fall of Soviet communism); the 1960s (space travel and global social movements); 1945 (the end of World War II and the dawn of nuclear energy); the nineteenth century (the Industrial Revolution and capitalism); and the sixteenth century (the European capture of the Americas and European settler colonialism in the Global South). In this model, globalization has a single origin located in Europe that can be identified as such.

The fourth and final historical framework is perhaps the trickiest of them all. Posing a single origin dating back centuries or even longer, this model nonetheless suggests that this origin marks the beginning of a *sequence of successive phases, stages*, or *ages of globalization*. Each of these phases is believed to contain origins

General Theories / 45

that should be seen as entirely new, but as *tipping points* of intensifying and accelerating interconnectivity and mobility. Hence, these periods are linked in linear rather than cyclical fashion.

Today, many generalizing globalization theorists subscribe to this phase model, albeit with some reservations. While emphasizing the significance of human interrelations that unfold over relatively long periods of time, they also recognize that human ties and mobilities have never been fashioned as quickly, intensely, and extensively as over the last century. After all, this recent acceleration dovetails with people's growing awareness of intensifying worldwide interconnectivities, which, in turn, led to the invention of the buzzword globalization.

In short, globalization may be an old dynamic, but it has undergone dramatic changes at specific *thresholds* in its history. Like a car transmission capable of switching into higher and lower gears, globalization crosses these historical tipping points that mark not only accelerating phases of global interconnectedness and mobility, but also unanticipated slowdowns and even reversals. Still, the prevailing view among generalizing thinkers who adopted the phase model is that such periods of stagnation could not permanently stop or reverse the forward movement of globalization.

If generalizing thinkers answer the question of globalization's historical origins according to the phase model, then what about their views on how to identify these discrete periods that define the evolution of globalization? To respond to this question, it is perhaps most fitting to turn to Roland Robertson, who made one of the earliest and most influential attempts to provide a historical periodization of globalization.

Robertson delineated his historical framework by following the conventional historical approach to periodize historical

46 / *General Theories*

> **Roland Robertson (1938–2022)** was a British social theorist who deserves the recognition of having been one of the first scholars to put globalization on the agenda of the social sciences. He held professorial positions in sociology at the University of Aberdeen (Scotland) and the University of Pittsburgh (USA). His influential definition of globalization emphasizes both objective social interconnectivity and subjective global consciousness. Strongly influenced by classical social thinkers like Durkheim and Parsons, who approached society as a system whose functions aimed at equilibrium and stability, Robertson attempted to conceive of the world in systemic terms as an interconnected "global field." Robertson was also one of the first social theorists to draw attention to the interpenetration of global and local scales. He popularized the term *glocalization* to indicate that, in the context of everyday social life, the macrodynamics of globalization always manifested in empirically measurable ways in their localized microsettings.

forces and events—in his case, to break up globalization into specific, identifiable phases. He realized that the work of historical periodization was central not only to the human effort to organize linear world-time but also to the determination of the social and cultural consequences of shrinking world-space. In the process of crafting a new general model that was more capable of integrating historical phenomena under the conceptual umbrella of globalization, Robertson found himself confronting two major conceptual challenges. The first was related to the problem of *vertical integration*: how to identify coherent patterns in the long sweep of past time? The second challenge involved *horizontal integration*: how to connect in each historical phase the broad range of human experiences around the world?[4]

Responding to this dual challenge, Robertson presents a periodization scheme he calls a *minimal phase model of globalization*.[5] It maps out five distinct historical phases covering more than five hundred years. Focusing primarily on relevant developments in Europe between the fifteenth and eighteenth centuries, he refers to this earliest stage as the *Germinal Phase*. It is framed by the European Enlightenment emphasis on ideas about humanity as a whole, as well as the development of scientific theories of the world as a planet. The second period, the *Incipient Phase*, is again set mostly in Europe, during the first half of the nineteenth century. It contains a significant shift toward the formation of unitary, homogeneous states linked to standardized, "nationalized" citizenry. The rise of the modern nation-state also entails the formalization of conceptions of "international relations."

Robertson calls the third period the *Take-Off Phase*. Ranging from the 1870s to the 1920s, it is characterized by a worldwide dynamic that favored more integrated forms of globalization and unified conceptions of humankind. Moreover, there is a sharp increase in the number and speed of global forms of communication such as the telegraph and the telephone. Finally, this phase also sees the first academic attempts to reflect on modernity as a new and unprecedented epoch in human history. Robertson names the fourth era of globalization rather awkwardly as the *Struggle-for-Hegemony Phase*. Extending from the 1920s to the 1960s, it entails a massive surge and worldwide extension of armed conflicts that were aptly referred to as "world wars" and "cold wars." It also witnesses the breakup of political alliances into three "worlds" or "blocs": the First World of Western democracies, the Second World of the Communist states, and the Third World of developing countries in the Global South.

Robertson completes his general historical periodization of globalization with the contemporary *Uncertainty Phase*. This era is characterized by the unprecedented intensification of global consciousness as well as a rapid acceleration in means of global communications enabled by the ICT Revolution. Connected to a greater fluidity of the international system, the number of international political and economic institutions as well as global social movements grow greatly. Public conceptions of individuals are rendered more diversified and complex by gender, sexual, ethnic, and racial considerations. At the same time, however, the Uncertainty Phase harbors proliferating ecological risks and social instabilities that threaten the survival of the planet as a whole.

When Robertson presented his minimal phase model in the early 1990s, it constituted a significant breakthrough in globalization theory. Most importantly, it challenged the dominant tendency in both the scholarly literature and popular representations to treat globalization as if it had only just emerged in the very recent past. Moreover, Robertson offered a sophisticated periodization framework of globalization that served as a useful foil for successive attempts to construct alternative models. Finally, his generalizing style of theorizing globalization not only inspired many historians to develop a new disciplinary subfield called *global history*, but also stimulated new research projects by cultural theorists who were relatively new to the subject of globalization.[6]

Still, there remain a number of problems with Robertson's minimal phase model, which makes it instructive to return to it in the concluding critical section of this chapter.

General Theories / 49

GLOBALIZING MODERNITY

In the context of globalization theory, Robertson's generalizing mode influenced social thinkers who embarked on related inquiries into the relationship between globalization and modernity. Indeed, *modernity* is perhaps the most important category in social theory that connects classical and contemporary macro-traditions. One of the most extensive and influential treatments of this modernity-globalization nexus is credited to the seminal study of Anthony Giddens, *The Consequences of Modernity* (1990). Let us examine its principal arguments as another illustration of how social thinkers theorize globalization in a generalizing style.

Giddens opens his analysis of the relationship between globalization and modernity with a definition of modernity as "modes of social life or organization, which emerged in Europe from about the seventeenth century onwards and which subsequently became more or less worldwide in their influence." Seemingly comfortable with locating his object of inquiry within a rather circumscribed Eurocentric framework, Giddens loses no time in advancing his even more controversial thesis. At its core, it amounts to a rejection of the notion of epochal change—a popular view in the neoliberal 1990s—proposing that humanity was entering the new era beyond modernity fueled by digital technology and free-market capitalist globalization. Giddens challenges this dominant perspective by insisting that "we are moving into one [era] in which the consequences of modernity are becoming more radicalized and universalized than before."[7]

To make a case for his thesis, the British thinker starts by challenging influential poststructuralist philosophers like François Lyotard and Jean Baudrillard, who had proclaimed the

> **Anthony Giddens (1938–)** is a notable British sociologist who taught for most of his academic life at the University of Cambridge, UK. He also served as an influential policy advisor to British prime minister Tony Blair in the late 1990s. In this capacity, he urged the Labour Party to consider a "Third Way" between socialism and capitalist liberalism. Subsequently, Giddens served as the director of the London School of Economics and Political Science from 1997 to 2003. In 2004, he was given life peerage as Lord Giddens in the British Upper House of Parliament, where he represents the Labour Party. Giddens's massive publication output encompasses more than thirty books and two hundred academic journal articles. These works cut across major areas of social inquiry such as social theory, history of social thought, environmental studies, nationalism, and the sociology of knowledge. Giddens was one of the first thinkers to theorize the relationship between globalization and modernity, arguing that globalization was not ending the modern era, but actually extending it.

birth of a *postmodern age* as the result of the alleged collapse of the foundational "metanarrative" of Enlightenment rationality steeped in notions of progress, liberation, and truth.[8] For Giddens, however, such postmodern critiques were based on the invention of trendy terms rather than engaging in a discerning analysis of modernity. If the term *postmodernism* was to mean anything at all, he argues, it should not be applied to social-scientific modes of inquiry. At best, it might serve as a loose descriptor of aesthetic aspects of social life, such as "styles and

General Theories / 51

movements within literature, painting, the plastic arts, and architecture."[9]

In short, Giddens posits the enduring significance of rational Enlightenment foundations of modernity, which are also necessary for the production of generalizable knowledge about contemporary social life. To strengthen his claim of the philosophical and historical continuity of modernity, he introduces the notion of *time-space distanciation*, which refers to the stretching of social interrelations across space and time.[10] For Giddens, time-space distanciation constitutes an intrinsic feature of modernity, which has greatly expanded and accelerated as a result of twentieth-century globalization. In premodern times, tribal and traditional communities tended to link time to a specific local place identified with natural occurrences such as the cyclical movement of ocean tides or celestial objects. Starting in Europe in the seventeenth century, however, time-space distanciation intensified dramatically and further accelerated with the Industrial Revolution and the formation of nation-states. Traditional localism gave way to the radical separation of time and space reflected, for example, in the introduction of abstract clock time and the corresponding uniformity in the social organization of time across large distances, such as the standardization of calendars and global time zones.

For Giddens, the modern reorganization of time and space involves both the speeding up of time reflected in the accelerated pace of social change and the expansion of space that brought different areas of the globe into permanent intercourse with one another. Modernity harbors two vital impulses—*restlessness* and *disposition to expand*—which are most clearly on display in the forces of rationalism, capitalism, and industrialism that have been radically transforming social life across the globe. Situated at the heart of modernity, time-space distanciation works hand in hand with what Giddens calls *disembedding mechanisms*—like the modern state, media networks, and transnational corporations. He takes the idea of modernity as disembedding from classical social thinkers like Max Weber and Talcott Parsons and applies it to globalization: the lifting of social relations out of their purely local interactions to be restructured across greater geographical and temporal distances.

Thus, Giddens asserts that these disembedding institutions of the twentieth century extended the scope of time-space distanciation. Connecting the global and the local in ways that would have been unthinkable in traditional societies, they affected the lives of billions of people worldwide. Disembedding processes also facilitated human *reflexivity*, understood as the production of generalizable knowledge about social life capable of traveling across vast spans of time-space and challenging the parochial fixities of traditional societies. Focusing his attention on the latest phase in this centuries-old expansionist dynamic, Giddens links modernization to what would become the buzzword of the 1990s: "We can interpret this process as one of *globalisation*, a term which must have a key position in the lexicon of the social sciences."[11]

What, then, is the precise relationship between modernity and globalization? At this point in our discussion, we can already anticipate Giddens's answer: "Modernity is inherently globalizing." In other words, the principal sources of the dynamism of modernity—time-space distanciation, disembedding, and reflexivity—and their corresponding social systems and institutions—primarily capitalism and the nation-state system—were capable of "tearing away" modernity from previous eras. By the end of the twentieth century, the intensity of time-space distanciation dwarfed that of earlier stages of modernity as relations between local and distant social forms and events had been stretched to the point where different localities and regions had become networked across the entire globe. As Giddens observes, the globalizing tendencies of modernity were actually *glocal* in that they connected "individuals to large-scale systems as part of complex dialectics of change at both local and global poles."[12]

At this point in his analysis, Giddens arrives at his influential definition of globalization: "Globalization can thus be defined as the intensification of worldwide social relations which link distant localities in such a way that local happenings are shaped by events occurring many miles away and vice versa."[13] This influential definition enshrines globalization as a continuous dynamic of modernity rather than an entirely new phenomenon. Rather than marking the end of modernity and the start of a new postmodern era, globalization actually constitutes one of the most significant *consequences of modernity*. Yet, Giddens concedes that the latest phase of modernization has become so intensified and extended that it calls out for new core concepts: *globalization* and *globalizing modernity*. After all, globalization processes represent the apex of modernity's inherent tendencies to radically reorganize time and space. Having reached this conclusion, Giddens renews his initial attack on postmodern thinkers whom he accuses of erroneously mislabeling various manifestations of globalizing modernity as a new and qualitatively distinct epoch of postmodernity in human history.[14]

Martin Albrow built his general globalization theory on the rejection of Anthony Giddens's thesis of globalizing modernity. Instead, he argued for an epochal shift from the *modern age* to the dawning *global age*. His generalizing analysis of the relationship between globalization and modernity opens with a criticism of

> **Martin Albrow (1937–)** is a prominent British sociologist, former president of the British Sociological Society, and Fellow of the British Academy of Social Sciences. In his principal work on globalization theory, *The Global Age: State and Society beyond Modernity* (1996), Albrow predicts the inevitable rise of a new *Global Age*, which will ultimately supplant the current era of late modernity. In 2022, Albrow created considerable controversy in Western academic circles by praising some aspects of the political ideology of Chinese president Xi Jinping as well as extolling China's role as a capable world leader.

the dominant view of modernity as a "time without end." In Albrow's view, this *totalizing discourse* in the social sciences has reduced all forms and manifestations of social change since the seventeenth century to mere additions to the modern age and thus made it exceedingly difficult for people to imagine a future era beyond modernity. Conversely, Albrow argues that the condition of modernity was actually running out of steam in the second half of the twentieth century as a result of globalization. He defines his keyword as a "multidimensional and open-ended set of processes" that powers today's gigantic social transformation. The outcome of globalization, he asserts, is the inevitable decline and ultimate fall of modernity and the rise of a new global age.

> Fundamentally, the Global Age involves the supplanting of modernity with globality and this means an overall change in the basis of action and social organization for individuals and groups. There are at least five major ways in which globality has taken us beyond

the assumptions of modernity. These include the global environmental consequences of aggregate human activities; the globality of communication systems; the rise of a global economy; and the reflexivity of globalism, where people and groups of all kinds refer to the globe as the frame for their beliefs.[15]

Reversing Giddens's critique of the postmodernist understanding of modernity, Albrow reproaches his colleague for misreading what is actually a manifestation of rupture as the continuation of modernity's global logic of expansion and intensification. Indeed, Giddens is accused of being incapable of breaking out of the totalizing conceptual framework of modernity that led him to commit a number of serious conceptual errors. First, Albrow argues that Giddens's thesis of modernity as inherently globalizing is both deterministic and teleological. It treats an outcome—globalization—as a necessary product of a process—modernity—as if modernity has fixed inner laws of development that set it on an inevitable course toward its predetermined goal. Albrow also notes that Giddens's obsession with the supposed inner logic of modernity prevents him from considering the emergence of new phenomena and circumstances that have the capacity of changing established modes in profound ways. What if modernity were actually an open-ended process capable of producing indeterminate outcomes that undermine its own tendencies? Might it then not be possible for human societies to move on to an era beyond modernity?

Moreover, Albrow finds his colleague's attachment to continuity in the modern age especially troubling in light of Giddens's own emphasis on the role of discontinuities and ruptures in giving birth to modernity in seventeenth-century Europe.[16] Giddens's inconsistent emphasis on discontinuity as applying only to the shift from traditional to modern societies also troubles other

56 / General Theories

general theorists who subscribe to an understanding of globalization as an evolutionary process driven by the development of social institutions on a planetary scale.[17]

Finally, Albrow asserts that Giddens's focus on the expansion of modernity eclipses the significance of contraction and limits under conditions of globalization. After all, forces of expansion associated with modernity might run up against the ultimate spatial limitation when the territory of the entire world is effectively enclosed. Albrow argues that it is people's growing recognition of the dangers of expansionism that forces them to pay more attention to the material *finitude* of the globe. The necessity of honoring especially the ecological limits nature imposes on human activities becomes ever more visible in a globalizing world subject to climate change and other global problems. The seriousness of global environmental problems requires people to break with modernity's logic of global expansion and intensification. As Albrow emphasizes, "Globality promotes the recognition of the limits of the earth but is profoundly different from modernity in that there is no presumption of centrality of control. The unification of the world which was the outcome of the Modern Project generates the common recognition that it has ended." Unlike the modern age, the global age becomes defined by central concerns of planetary finitude and human limits that arrest the expansionistic dynamic of modernity. Hence, Albrow concludes that "globalization, far from being the end to which human beings have aspired, is the termination of modern ways of organizing life which they took for granted. The global shift is a transformation, not a culmination."[18]

If Albrow's thesis is correct, then, far from being the latest stage in a long process of modern development, the global age actually constitutes a new era in history. It has arisen from a combination of different forces that have unexpectedly terminated the course of modernity by setting worldwide limits and creating alternatives to its supposedly "inherent" tendencies and institutions. And these limits cannot be overcome from within this logic of modernity. Accordingly, Albrow offers a provocative inversion of Giddens's thesis: rather than embracing the idea that modernity is inherently globalizing, globality is "inherently demodernizing."[19] The assumptions underlying Albrow's new formula of demodernizing globality also point to another flaw in Giddens's theory: the primacy of quantity over quality. Conceptualizing globalization in terms of "expansion" and "intensification" of existing modern social institutions and arrangements—primarily capitalism and the nation-state system—Giddens misses the significance of profound qualitative shifts reflected in newly emergent social forms and forces such as the rise of the digital network society or the transnationalization of capital that destabilizes the exclusive territoriality of the modern nation-state.

Ultimately, both Giddens's and Albrow's conflicting approaches proved to be highly influential not only for generalizing globalization theorists, but also for social thinkers interested in particular dimensions of globalization or modernity.

MAPPING GLOBALIZATION

There are only a handful of social thinkers who accepted the formidable challenge of employing a general mode of theorizing to construct a general analytical framework of globalization.[20] Towering among them, one can find David Held and his collaborators Anthony McGrew, an international relations scholar who interpreted domestic politics as a product of powerful interstate forces; David Goldblatt, a social theorist with a strong

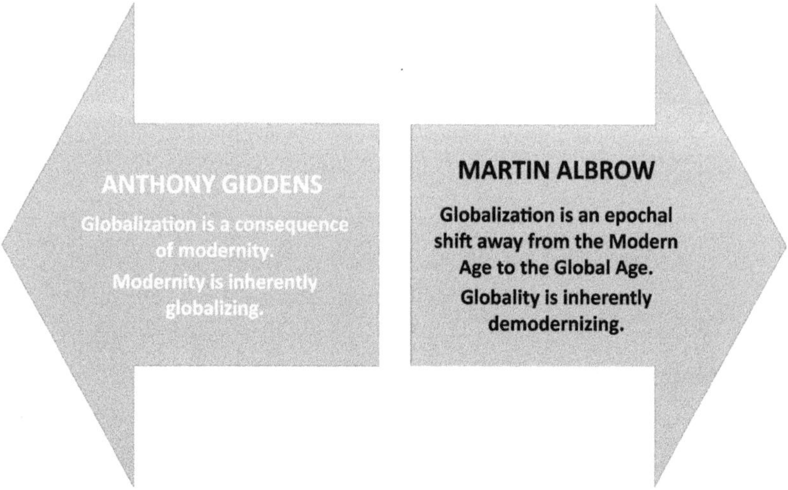

58 / General Theories

Figure 6. Globalization and modernity: Giddens versus Albrow

background in ecology and environmental policy; and Jonathan Perraton, a noted economist and international finance expert. To give another illustration of the generalizing mode of theorizing, let us consider their comprehensive attempt to map globalization in all its dimensions. Its primary features can be found in their pathbreaking five-hundred-page study, *Global Transformations* (1999), which was the outcome of an entire decade of collaborative and transdisciplinary globalization research.

The generalizing mode of inquiry utilized by Held and his collaborators (from here forward referred to as Held) unfolds in a series of five conceptual steps that contain the key components of their globalization theory. The first step starts with Held's firm rejection of dominant accounts of globalization as a dynamic anchored primarily in the economic domain. Instead, he describes the compression of world-space and world-time as

General Theories / 59

> **David Held (1951–2019)** was a widely cited British political and social theorist. He was the cofounder of the prominent academic publishing house Polity Press (Cambridge, UK). Held taught for most of his academic career at the London School of Economics and Durham University. His extensive scholarly work covers topics in critical theory, cosmopolitan democracy, global governance, and ecological sustainability. Held was one of the first globalization theorists to attempt a comprehensive mapping of globalization processes, which he intended to be historically grounded as well as informed by a rigorous and generally applicable analytical framework.

a highly differentiated set of processes that unfold across six distinct aspects of social activity: economics, politics, culture, military, migration, and ecology. This multidimensional approach makes it easier for Held to present globalization as a *multicausal process* involving a combination of social forces including technological innovation, market dynamics, ideology, and political decisions. In other words, his generalizing mode seeks to overcome monocausal explanations that point to a single dimension of social activity—usually economics or politics—as the source of global transformation. Finally, this initial step also underscores the significance of interconnectivity and mobility as key qualities of globalization.

Held's second move involves the location of his approach within the academic context of the globalization debates of the late 1990s. To that end, he presents globalization theorists belonging to the antagonistic camps of *hyperglobalizers*, *skeptics*, and *transformationalists*. Since we are already familiar with this framework from the introduction, there is no need to go into further detail here. While Held shows some sympathy for the transformationalist camp, he rejects its overly deterministic depictions of global transformation toward a fixed historical destination such as a single world society or a globally integrated market. Instead, Held subscribes to a more contingent version of transformationalism that casts globalization as an uncertain and open-ended set of processes susceptible to unanticipated setbacks and reversals.

Held's third step in his macro-mapping process entails the identification of four spatiotemporal forms of globalization: the *extensity* or width of global networks; the *intensity* or depth of global interconnectedness; the *velocity* or speed of global flows; and the *impact propensity* of global interconnectedness. While breadth, depth, and speed appear to be straightforward criteria for evaluating globalization, impact propensity is a trickier category and thus requires further elaboration. Ultimately, Held distinguishes between four types of impact: *decisional*, understood as the impact of globalization on policy options and social choices; *institutional*, referring to the impact of globalization on organizational agendas and designs; *distributive*, defined as the impact of globalization on the distribution of power and wealth within and between countries; and *structural*, understood as the impact of globalization on major political and economic structures such as states and capitalist markets.

In addition to these four spatiotemporal dimensions—extensity, intensity, velocity, and impact—Held's fourth step involves the introduction of four *organizational dimensions*. First, physical, legal, and symbolic *infrastructures* are necessary for facilitating global connections and flows. Second, the *institutionalization* of global networks requires the regulation and routini-

General Theories / 61

zation of global patterns of interconnectedness in terms of trade pacts, defense alliances, sports events, and so on. Third, globalization is also organized through patterns of *social stratification* that reflect uneven and asymmetrical class and power relations. Finally, dominant *modes of interaction* ranging from coercion to cooperation are responsible for the rise and fall of specific globalization regimes across various historical epochs.

Comprised of no fewer than *eight key components*—four spatio-temporal dimensions and four organizational dimensions—Held's sprawling analytical map of globalization constitutes the basis for qualitative and quantitative assessments of its historical patterns that can be measured empirically. Moreover, Held's systematic evaluation of how these eight key components have played out across centuries allows for a sophisticated historical comparison of distinctive *types of globalization* and a sharper identification of their key attributes.

Held and his collaborators are now ready to put the finishing touches on their holistic analytical mapping of globalization. Accordingly, their fifth and last conceptual step involves the construction of a comprehensive *typology of globalization.* It consists of four discrete globalization categories, which reflect different macropatterns of worldwide flows, networks, mobilities, and interactions. *Type 1* constitutes what Held calls *thick globalization.* It is characterized by the extensive reach of global networks that is matched by their high levels of intensity, high speed, and high impact across all domains and organizational dimensions of social life. One concrete manifestation of Type 1 globalization is the deregulated 1990s turbocapitalist world advocated by market globalists, in which national borders have become porous and thus less relevant.

On the opposite end of the spectrum, we find *Type 4*. It qualifies as *thin globalization* because it contains global networks that

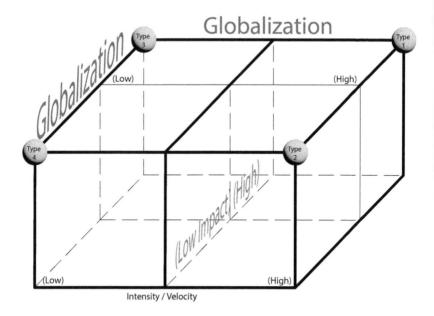

Type 1 = Thick globalization
(high extensity, high intensity, high velocity, high impact)
Type 2 = Diffused globalization
(high extensity, high intensity, high velocity, low impact)
Type 3 = Expansive globalization
(high extensity, low intensity, low velocity, high impact)
Type 4 = Thin globalization
(low extensity, low intensity, low velocity, low impact)

Figure 7. David Held's general globalization theory

rank low on all eight key components of globalization. This type corresponds to a deglobalized world of reinvigorated, sovereign nation-states invoked by national populists. *Types 2 and 3* are located between these thick and thin models. They correspond to *diffused* (Type 2) and *expansive* (Type 3) forms of globalization. *Diffused globalization* ranks high on the scale of extensity, intensity, and velocity, but its impact is highly mediated by national or global institutions. This form of globalization resonates with the vision of justice globalists who embrace the idea of a highly

General Theories / 63

interconnected world whose social impacts are tightly regulated by egalitarian institutions of global governance. *Expansive globalization* scores high on the criteria of extensity and impact, but low on intensity and velocity. This type is exemplified in the bygone world of Western colonial empires whose violent and exploitative practices negatively impacted indigenous peoples.

While Held and his collaborators clearly employ a generalizing style of theorizing to produce their comprehensive globalization map, they also show some affinity for the complexity mode. Still, they insist that their extremely intricate and differentiated mapping of globalizing processes be grasped in its totality only through an overarching framework attentive to the complex dynamics operating in multiple dimensions. Thus, their research aim is to develop a holistic, yet often maddingly abstract, explanation of globalization, which highlights the interactions between a multiplicity of social forces that drive the worldwide transformations of our time.[21] Despite some limitations discussed below, Held and his collaborators came closer than any previous attempt to presenting a systematic and integrated theory of globalization.

CONCLUDING CRITICAL REFLECTIONS

As we discussed, the generalizing mode of theorizing globalization possesses a number of virtues. First, it develops a general and systematic framework for understanding the compression of the world in its social totality. Scholars writing in this mode keep alive the possibility of assembling a big picture of globalization that contains all of its major components and also explains how the process unfolds across a wide range of domains and geographical and historical contexts. Second, generalizing

64 / *General Theories*

thinkers build their models of globalization on long-standing currents of social thought whose intellectual achievements have withstood the test of time. Indeed, all of the thinkers introduced in this chapter draw on insights presented in the works of classical social thinkers like Karl Marx, Max Weber, and Émile Durkheim. Thus, the generalizing mode of inquiry enriches globalization theory by linking it to the principal categories and issues of modern social thought.

On the downside, however, general theories of globalization are overly abstract and remain attached to classical concepts and debates of nineteenth- and twentieth-century European social theory. As we noted, this strong affinity means that the problems and shortcomings of classical social theory are imported into globalization theory as well. For example, most generalizing globalization thinkers follow in the footsteps of classical European thinkers by showing only limited interest in addressing crucial contemporary identity categories such as race, gender, sexual orientation, and so on. In addition, references to recent perspectives in postcolonial and indigenous theory or other relevant non-Western frameworks are sporadic and often underdeveloped. If they do occur, these engagements with Global South perspectives are usually confined to overly defensive responses to legitimate demands for the greater incorporation of knowledge produced outside the Euro-American academy.

As pointed out, Anthony Giddens links his key concept of modernity—which he uses in the singular—to specific European historical contexts and geographic origins. It should not surprise us that his understanding of globalization as the corollary of Western modernity incensed postcolonial thinkers as well as postmodern theorists. Does this mean, as some of these critics charge, that Giddens's idea of globalization as the con-

General Theories / 65

tinuation of preestablished European paths is hopelessly mired in Eurocentrism?[22] To be fair to Giddens, let us consider his rejoinder, which comes in two parts. First, he argues that modernity and globalization are indeed Western projects with respect to their *geographic origin* and *disembedding institutions* such as industrial capitalism and the nation-state system. At the same time, however, Giddens is careful to point out that, by the end of the twentieth century, the expansionist dynamics of European modernity had robbed the Occident of its exclusive control of the process. From the standpoint of its *globalizing tendencies* rather than its origin, he argues, modernity is thus not particularly Western, because it has by now become an integral dynamism of all regions and cultures on the planet.

Hence, while acknowledging the violent role of European imperialism and colonialism in the process of globalizing modernity, Giddens also recognizes its future-oriented, open-ended trajectory. In his view, globalization generates incessantly new forms of *world interdependence* and *planetary consciousness* that involve conceptions and strategies influenced by non-Western settings. Still, his view of European modernity as universalizing—both in its global impact and in its accumulation of reflexive knowledge—locks Giddens into the controversial, and not easily defendable, position that universality actually contains at its core the European scientific method and rationality, which ultimately ride roughshod over cultural specificity. As Giddens puts it, "Discursive argumentation, including that which is constitutive of natural science, involves criteria that override cultural differentiations."[23]

Ultimately, Giddens's defense thesis of globalization as a consequence of modernity fails to extricate itself fully from the charge of Eurocentrism. Moreover, it neither acknowledges nor engages alternative theories that advocate more than one path of modernization. For example, leading proponents of the *multiple modernities model*, such as the social theorist Shmuel Eisenstadt, have long criticized Eurocentric frameworks of development for their inability to recognize that the impact of European modernity on non-Western societies did not preclude them from fashioning their own trajectories of modernity that were often quite different from the original.[24] In the same vein, global studies scholars like Jan Nederveen Pieterse charge Giddens with failing to consider the ongoing formation of new "mélange modernities" in various parts of the world. Hence, globalization processes not only spawned multiple modernities but also greatly encouraged the creation and expansion of new hybrid combinations of traditional and modern social practices.[25]

General theory's overemphasis on the role of Europe as the originating source of globalization also plagues Robertson's periodization outline, which remains largely a prisoner of Eurocentric stage models of history. After all, it infers a determined path of historical development whose major periods such as the Take-Off Phase are associated with Western forms of market-based development theory.[26] Robertson also seems to confuse the necessary act of periodizing history with the naming of dominant formations of globalization at particular historical junctures. To be sure, it is important to delineate crucial phases and put dates around them. But the backward-looking naming of such epochs from the current historical era reflects a problematic tendency in globalization theory: *presentism.* This term refers to the problematic tendency of focusing too narrowly on contemporary times and reading the past from the standpoint of the present. As globalization scholar Jan Nederveen Pieterse observes, "because of its presentist leanings, much research treats globalization unre-

General Theories / 67

flexively, may overlook structural patterns, present as novel what are older features, and misread contemporary trends."[27]

Presentism also appears in Robertson's and Giddens's historical frameworks in its related form of *epochalism*. This concept applies to the intellectual fallacy of believing that the present time represents an unprecedented new era whose patterns are vastly different from prior epochs. For example, Robertson's Uncertainty Phase creates the false impression that the current manifestation of uncertainty lacks historical precedents. To be sure, the twenty-first century shows significant levels of uncertainty and volatility.[28] But different forms of unsettling also emerged in the past, often as a result of large-scale warfare such as the Mongol expansion in the thirteenth century or as the consequence of pandemics such as measles and smallpox that spread rapidly from European invaders to Native American populations. Generalizing globalization thinking thrives on claims of novelty by paying far more attention to human advances in Europe during the last few centuries mostly related to industrial technology and capitalist economics than to non-Western achievements such as the domestication of the horse or the invention of writing. This dual stranglehold of presentism and epochalism feeds into the still-dominant Eurocentric narrative according to which globalization did not start until the rise of the West and the Industrial Revolution, conventionally dated between 1500 and 1800.

Even pioneering globalization theorists like Roland Robertson and Anthony Giddens who subscribed to the phase model of globalization largely remained prisoners of linear modernization theories that overemphasize the role of Europe and North America as both the sources and drivers of world-historical dynamics and events. Such perspectives reveal their deep embeddedness in what historian James Blaut refers to as the *colonizer's model of the world*.[29] These biased frameworks reveal that phase models that cover only a few centuries are bound to fall into the trap of Eurocentrism. However, if we revise our historical approach to globalization by extending its origins to much longer periods of time, the picture changes dramatically. For example, stretching the phases of globalization across millennia reveals that Homo sapiens became a truly global species as far back as 10,000 BCE when small nomadic bands of hunter-gatherers reached the southernmost tip of South America. This crowning achievement of human mobility brought to a successful completion a series of prior terrestrial walkabouts by African hominins at least two million years ago. In short, long-term revisions of the phase model correct the overemphasis on Europe by opening our eyes to a more accurate understanding of globalization as a lengthy *multicentric* and *multidirectional* process emanating at different times from multiple civilizational hubs located on all continents.[30]

A final weakness of the generalizing mode of theorizing globalization is that it requires the preliminary task of mapping out in much detail the various domains of the phenomenon, which then are brought back together in highly abstract overarching models. This onerous task of conceptual (re)construction requires generalizing theorists to engage in significant violence of abstraction by removing their constructs from directly observable dynamics in order to create the necessary space for their assemblage of holistic analytical frameworks. As reflected in Held's macro-mapping exercise, the attempt to present multi-dimensionality within a unified macro framework ultimately leads to a confusing sprawl of analytical categories and typologies like *spatiotemporal dimensions* or *organizational dimensions*.

Piling abstractions upon abstractions, generalizing thinkers find themselves bogged down in lengthy explanations of how these proliferating constructs fit together. Moreover, the task of explaining multiple relationships among a large number of phenomena often neglects the uniqueness of each phenomenon to which these ideas refer. As a result, the proliferating conceptual vocabulary of general theory lacks specificity. This makes empirical testing rather difficult as well as reducing the explanatory power of the theoretical analysis.[31]

Similarly, when applied to specific global problems such as climate change or economic inequality, the distinctions between these high-order categories become blurred, thus inviting conceptual confusion and frustration. Hence, we should keep in mind that the generalizing mode of theorizing of globalization is vulnerable to criticism concerning its ability to explain the concrete dynamics of global interconnectivity, mobility, and imagination without losing itself in generalizations and abstractions. And it is to these more specific and particular ways of theorizing globalization as it unfolds in its major social dimensions or domains to which we now turn.

NOTES

1. Jan Nederveen Pieterse, "Rethinking Modernity and Capitalism," *sociopedia.isa* (2014), 2.

2. C. Wright Mills, *The Sociological Imagination* (Oxford, UK: Oxford University Press, 2000).

3. George Ritzer and Paul Dean, *Globalization: A Basic Text*, 2nd ed. (Oxford, UK: Wiley Blackwell, 2015), 31–38.

4. David Northrup, "Globalization and the Great Convergence: Rethinking World History in the Long Term," *Journal of World History* 16, no. 3 (2005): 249.

5. Roland Robertson, *Globalization: Social Theory and Global Culture* (London: Sage, 1992), 57–60.

6. See Sebastian Conrad, *What Is Global History?* (Princeton, NJ: Princeton University Press, 2017); John Tomlinson, *Globalization and Culture* (Chicago: University of Chicago Press, 1999).

7. Anthony Giddens, *The Consequences of Modernity* (Stanford, CA: Stanford University Press, 1990), 1–3.

8. François Lyotard, *The Postmodern Condition: A Report on Knowledge* (Minneapolis: University of Minnesota Press, 1984), 3.

9. Giddens, *Consequences of Modernity*, 45.

10. Giddens, 20.

11. Giddens, 52–53.

12. Giddens, 177.

13. Giddens, 64.

14. Giddens, 177.

15. Martin Albrow, *The Global Age: State and Society beyond Modernity* (Stanford, CA: Stanford University Press, 1996), 4.

16. Albrow, 99–101.

17. George Modelski, Tessaleno Devezas, and William R. Thompson, eds., *Globalization as Evolutionary Process: Modeling Global Change* (London: Routledge, 2008), 11–18.

18. Albrow, *Global Age*, 100, 192.

19. Albrow, 99.

20. Among these thinkers are David Held, Roland Robertson, Jan-Aart Scholte, and George Modelski.

21. David Held, Anthony McGrew, David Goldblatt, and Jonathan Perraton, eds., *Global Transformations* (Cambridge, UK: Polity Press, 1999), 12.

22. See, for example, Jan Nederveen Pieterse, *Globalization & Culture: Global Mélange*, 3rd ed. (Lanham, MD: Rowman & Littlefield, 2015), 69.

23. Giddens, *Consequences of Modernity*, 175–76.

24. See, for example, Shmuel N. Eisenstadt, ed., *Multiple Modernities* (New Brunswick, NJ: Transaction Books, 2002).

25. Pieterse, *Globalization & Culture*, 172.

26. Roland Robertson has since revised this conception and has done a lot of work on ideas of globalization during the classical empires of antiquity as well as non-European civilizations, thus pushing his

schema back to more than two thousand years ago. See, for example, Robertson, "Beyond the Discourse of Globalization," *Glocalism: A Journal of Culture, Politics and Innovation* 1 (2015): 1–14.

27. Jan Nederveen Pieterse, "Periodizing Globalization: Histories of Globalization," *New Global Studies* 6, no. 2 (2012): 1.

28. See Manfred B. Steger and Paul James, *Globalization Matters: Engaging the Global in Unsettled Times* (Cambridge, UK: Cambridge University Press, 2019).

29. James Blaut, *The Colonizer's Model of the World: Geographical Diffusionism and Eurocentric History* (New York: Guilford Press, 2021).

30. Pieterse, "Periodizing Globalization," 1–15.

31. Shelby D. Hunt, "General Theories and the Fundamental Explananda of Marketing," *Journal of Marketing* 47 (Fall 1983): 11–12.

CHAPTER TWO

Domain Theories

This chapter presents an overview of influential theories of globalization crafted in a domain style of inquiry. After our initial explanation of domain theory and its primary features, we explore this mode of thinking in more detail by focusing on three major dimensions of globalization.

We start with economic relations as theorized by neoliberal thinkers like Theodore Levitt and Thomas Friedman as well as neo-Marxist scholars like William Robinson in their important writings. While approaching their subject from different methodological and ideological positions, their theories nonetheless converge in their common focus on the significance of *globalizing capitalism* and its main actors. Next, we turn to the political domain of globalization as presented in the writings of Jan Aart Scholte and of Michael Hardt and Antonio Negri. Their innovative evaluations of globalization as a force shaping new forms of territoriality and sovereignty address the changing *role of the state in a globalizing world*. This discussion of the transformation of political spaces is followed by a consideration of cultural globalization, especially as reflected in Jan Nederveen Pieterse's innovative approach. Challenging the two opposing dominant theses on the subject—*clashing cultural differences* and *intensifying cultural sameness*—the Dutch theorist sees cultural globalization instead as a process driving the production and worldwide dissemination of novel *hybrid* symbolic forms.

In addition to sharing a special affinity for domain thinking, the scholars presented in this chapter also employ some of the other modes of theorizing discussed in the introduction. Documenting their ability to employ multiple styles serves as an important corrective to the necessary *analytical* separation of distinct styles of thinking. The chapter ends with a critical evaluation of the major strengths and weaknesses of the domain mode of theorizing globalization.

THE DOMAIN MODE OF THEORIZING

Domain theory is a conceptual category that encompasses phenomena and dynamics occurring in clearly demarcated dimensions of society. In our concrete lifeworlds, however, these abstractly outlined domains overlap and intersect in multiple and complex ways. Still, the delineation and investigation of distinct parts makes for a greater appreciation of the enormous scale of social relations.

Different versions of domain theory have been developed in several academic fields that cut across the natural and social sciences. In mathematics, for example, domain theory refers to the study of partially ordered sets of elements or numbers. In computer science, it is used to outline functional programming languages. In linguistics, it supports the study of semantics—spoken meanings—in different social contexts. And in social psychology, domain thinkers focus on morality as a distinct dimension of social life in order to examine how children and young adults acquire normative understandings of fairness, rights, and social justice.

In social theory, the domain style of inquiry is often linked to mid-level approaches that seek to balance theory and empirical research. In the 1960s, the American social theorist Robert K. Merton coined the term *middle-range theory* to refer to such mixed approaches. He suggests that the necessary task of theory-building should start with empirical data related to specific aspects of social life, but ultimately aim at more general statements about the chosen domain. As Merton explains, "Sociological theory, if it is to advance significantly, must proceed on these interconnected planes: (1) by developing special theories from which to derive hypotheses that can be empirically investigated, and (2) by evolving a progressively more general conceptual scheme that is adequate to consolidate groups of special theories."[1]

Engaged in the development of such special theories, most domain thinkers of globalization are skeptical about the utility of building macro theories of worldwide interdependence based on a general pattern operating across all major dimensions. Approaching globalization as a differentiated set of processes, they proceed in two stages. The first step consists of assembling a comprehensive lay of the land that identifies the most pivotal domains of the space-time compression. Second, domain thinkers carve up the enormity of global interconnectivity into more digestible pieces and then limit their analysis to one or, at most, two globalization dimensions.

Unsurprisingly, the domain style of inquiry has attracted scholars trained in conventional disciplines and eager to apply their particular expertise to the study of globalization. The most frequently researched dimensions include *economic relations*, referring to the intensification and stretching of economic connections across the globe; *political* and *governmental relations*, dealing with expansion and acceleration of political and governance relations across the world; *cultural relations*, exploring the stretching and intensification of cultural flows across the globe; *ideological relations*, tackling the worldwide expansion and transformation of political belief systems; and *technological relations*, examining the role of new digital technologies in creating a more interconnected world. As we explore in more detail in chapter 5, the rapid acceleration of climate change in the twenty-first century, in particular, has spawned new efforts to theorize ecological globalization.

Over the years, new domains and subdomains have been added to this expanding list. These include ecology, communications, media, art, law, religion, democracy, education, military and warfare, race and ethnicity, gender and feminism, human rights, diplomacy, social movements, citizenship, postcolonialism, urbanization, security, surveillance, migration, and many more. As a result of the proliferation of such domain approaches, several substantive book series on globalization have appeared in major languages, containing many volumes that cover a broad spectrum of the phenomenon.[2] Let us, then, turn to three of the most widely theorized dimensions of globalization to illustrate the domain mode through the works of influential thinkers.

DISSECTING GLOBAL CAPITALISM

The *economic dimension of globalization* constitutes the most popular subject of the earliest theoretical writings on the subject. Various thinkers have explored in much detail how the expansion of the economy has given rise to new and intensified forms of global interdependence.[3] Many theories are built upon an actor-oriented approach that shines the analytical spotlight on the growth of transnational corporations (TNCs) like Walmart and Apple; the impact of post–World War II international economic institutions like the World Trade Organization (WTO), the International Monetary Fund (IMF), and the World Bank; and the development of global banking and finance, especially in the wake of the devastating 2008 Global Financial Crisis. Typically, these theories break up the macrostructures of the global economy into its major components, which makes it easier to study the major economic actors in isolation from each other. This method contributes to a better understanding of their particular significance in the complex circuits of global production and finance networks operating according to the rules and conventions of the worldwide capitalist market system.[4]

As we discussed in the introduction, the dominant discourse at the turn of the twenty-first century linked the meaning of globalization to the neoliberal economic agenda of the expansion of *free trade* and the global integration of *free markets* powered by the ICT revolution. Over the last decades, the neoliberal revolution spread to all corners of the world, including the former Soviet bloc and reform-minded Communist China.[5] It aimed at nothing less than the wholesale replacement of the dominant postwar paradigm of Keynesian regulated capitalism. The neoliberal wave also pushed globalization theorists closer to considering the economic domain of worldwide interconnectivity. Although supporters and detractors of neoliberalism occupied opposing ends of the ideological spectrum, their attention nonetheless converged thematically on dissecting the principal features and dynamics of global capitalism.

Domain Theories / 77

As early as the 1980s, Harvard University's Business School dean Theodore Levitt offered a highly influential theory of neoliberal capitalism. His analysis is based on what he considers to be "indisputable empirical trends" in the development of the globalizing economic system. The thrust of his argument suggests that TNCs have no choice but to operate in a cost-effective way by standardizing their products across national markets. Only the swift adoption of such a global approach would keep them profitable through the elimination of expensive adjustments to multiple national markets. In other words, Levitt claims that CEOs and other corporate leaders must think and act "as if the world were one large market—ignoring superficial regional and national differences ... It [the global corporation] sells the same things in the same way everywhere." This imperative of worldwide economic homogenization along the lines of Anglo-American neoliberal capitalism also frames Levitt's depiction of globalization as an "inevitable" and "irreversible" economic process.[6]

Two decades later, the widely read *New York Times* syndicated columnist Thomas Friedman consciously drew on Levitt's neoliberal framework to define globalization as the "inexorable integration of markets, nation-states, and technologies to a degree never witnessed before." Advocating the restructuring of public enterprises and the privatization of key industrial sectors, Friedman asserts that globalization has its own set of economic rules that revolve around opening, deregulating, and privatizing the economy. *Market* represents *the* core concept in Friedman's theory of global capitalism, which equates one specific domain of globalization—economic relations—with the entire process: "The relevant market today is the planet Earth and the global integration of technology, finance, trade, and information." For

Friedman, globalization is both a new phase in the unfolding of modernity and an objective, interconnected system. Possessing an all-encompassing structure and logic, the neoliberal economic rules of the globalization system "today directly or indirectly influence the politics, environment, geopolitics and economics of virtually every country in the world."[7]

Equally important theoretical inquiries into global capitalism also stem from critics of neoliberal capitalism. Some of these thinkers were originally associated with *world-systems theory*—a generic label for neo-Marxist explanations of worldwide economic change originating in sixteenth-century Europe.[8] These theorists outlined a single *world-system* rooted in basic structural components of the world economy. They argued that the system was driven by the extractive logic of capital accumulation that combined with imperialist Western practices of economic exploitation. Thus, the worldwide expansion of capitalism produced economic equality that divided the rich *core* in the Global North from the exploited *periphery* in the Global South. Still, the original designers of world-systems theory have remained critical of globalization theory. Arguing that the modern capitalist economy has been global since its inception five centuries ago, they consider globalization an inflated term, which constitutes neither a new organizing concept for understanding the world economy nor an explanatory framework for the evolution of global capitalism.[9]

Ironically, some thinkers previously associated with world-systems theory have abandoned their old framework and turned to globalization theory. They insist that globalization is a useful organizing concept that opens the door to the creation of new perspectives on neoliberal capitalism. Accessible and yet sophisticated, William Robinson's writings on the subject are a lucid

> **William I. Robinson (1959–)** is a professor of sociology, global studies, Latin American studies, and political economy at the University of California, Santa Barbara. A former investigative journalist, Robinson has long since emerged as a prominent scholar-activist who attempts to link his academic work to political struggles for social justice and participatory democracy around the world. His writings are especially significant and innovative in that they proceed in a critical dialogue with both world-systems theory and other neo-Marxist currents such as Antonio Gramsci's perspective. At the same time, Robinson has developed an original domain approach to globalization, which he calls the *global capitalism approach.*

example of how the domain mode of theorizing economic globalization can be employed from a neo-Marxist perspective that is deeply critical of the neoliberal interpretive framework assembled by Levitt and Friedman.

For Robinson, the latest phase of globalization has ushered in an *epochal shift* in the history of capitalism. Although its current form remains defined by the same accumulation imperative of earlier stages of capitalism, it has crossed a threshold by "going global." True to a domain mode of thinking, Robinson links globalization to the rise of *transnational capital* and the related integration of every country into a globalized system of production, finance, and services.[10] In other words, the defining feature of economic globalization is transnational capital and the global mobility of investment flows, both of which have been greatly enhanced by the current neoliberal framework. In today's transnational phase, the capitalist system has moved from what Robinson calls a *world economy* based on *national* circuits of production and accumulation to an overarching *global economy* based on global circuits of production and accumulation, in which products and services can no longer be considered as national in any meaningful way.[11] This means that economic globalization is not merely a *quantitative* intensification of capitalism's historical tendencies to expand and accelerate, but also a *qualitatively* new stage characterized by the deep integration of economic production and extensive trade infrastructures driven by economic globalization.

As an example, Robinson cites the enhanced ability of TNCs to *outsource manufacturing jobs.* This practice has delivered greater corporate profits through the cutting of labor costs achieved by the dispersal of the economic production process into many discrete phases and carried out by low-wage workers in the Global South. Another example is the ability of TNCs to cultivate interconnected relationships with many other companies of various sizes and types. It is through the spinning of such sprawling economic webs that even small firms and financial agents in a single country can become directly linked to a global production network.[12] Finally, Robinson points out that transnational capital is not just about assets located in the northern hemisphere. It also includes powerful TNCs in the Global South such as the Brazilian-based conglomerate Vale, one of the world's largest mining companies, and the Indian-based car giant Tata Motors.

Hence, the study of the economic domain of globalization often involves theoretical inquiries into its constitutive parts and elements. Among the most important of these are worldwide production networks whose globally dispersed nodes add significant value to the production and distribution of goods and services. Such *global value chains* (GVCs) allow TNCs like Apple, Bank of America, and General Motors to connect firms, workers, and consumers around the world and market their products and services on a global scale. Given their indispensable status in the global economy, GVCs constitute a popular subject among domain thinkers of economic globalization. Such theories tend to be empirically oriented and focus on the composition and evolution of GVCs in a variety of industrial sectors such as commodities, apparel, electronics, and tourism. Pioneering economic sociologists like Gary Gereffi and economic geographers like Peter Dicken have designed sophisticated analytical GVC frameworks that enhance our understanding of how industries and economic enterprises have been organized in the age of globalization.[13]

Incorporating GVCs as a key component into his model, Robinson takes his theory of global capitalism into new terrain by linking economic globalization to the rise of two related social formations on the global level. The first is the *transnational capitalist class* (TCC), which is primarily made up of the owners and managers of TNCs. The second is the *transnational state apparatus* (TNS), through which the TCC attempts to convert the power of the global capitalist economy into a transnational political authority structure.[14] Robinson observes that the interests of these global elites lie primarily in the promotion of global circuits of accumulation, which prepares the ground for the massive expansion of TNCs around the world. In order to aid their neoliberal efforts to open the world to transnational capital, the TCC promotes and draws on cutting-edge computer and information technology. Although Robinson acknowledges the importance of digital technology, he nonetheless rejects Friedman's causal argument that the ICT revolution drives

Figure 8. William Robinson's theory of global capitalism

economic globalization. Conversely, Robinson points to the economic drive of global capitalism to maximize corporate profits as the primary cause fueling the invention and application of new technologies.[15]

Turning his analysis to the TNS, Robinson finds that it functions as a collective authority of the TCC to exercise its power in individual countries and the global capitalist system as a whole. But he cautions that the TNS should not be considered a "world government." Rather, it serves as an analytical concept that refers to loose networks of transnational capital interwoven with national governments and transnational institutions. For example, the TNS works through institutions like the IMF and the World Bank, which impose neoliberal *structural adjustment programs* on the Global South. These obligatory measures consist of market-oriented policies that governments of poor countries must implement in exchange for much-needed economic development loans. Yet, Robinson observes that such steamrolling of neoliberal policies creates serious social problems such as growing economic inequality, environmental degradation, political instability, and military conflicts. In order to protect continuous capitalist expansion, the TNS must resolve these self-created problems, often by resorting to authoritarian methods that, in the short term, seem to make it easier to control popular resistance in the form of anticapitalist social movements.

However, the inevitable by-product of the successful suppression of dissent might be the mushrooming of the TNS into an antidemocratic *global police state*, whose primary task would be the worldwide spread and protection of unregulated markets through myriad forms of intimidation and violence. By global police state, Robinson means a growing political system of warfare and militarization, mass social control including imprisonment, surveillance, and repression. In short, the global police state aims to contain potential resisters and criminalize resistance. Hence, Robinson warns that the increasing dependence of global capitalism on the global police state could bring about a worldwide "sharp turn toward twenty-first-century fascism, the fusion of reactionary political power with transnational capital."[16]

By theorizing these crucial connections between globalized capitalism, economic control, and political domination, Robinson's economic domain thinking crosses over into the dimension of political globalization, which we shall consider next.

RETHINKING TERRITORIALITY AND SOVEREIGNTY

Our discussion in the previous section has revealed that economic globalization can hardly be theorized apart from an analysis of power relations and political institutions. Accordingly, a second popular topic examined by domain theorists of globalization involves *politics* and *governance*, especially as these relate to the worldwide transformation of political spaces. One question often tops the research agenda of globalization theorists: do growing transnational flows and interconnectivities pose a serious threat to the conventional powers of the nation-state?

No doubt, this question implies that economic globalization, in particular, might be the chief culprit that negatively affects the ability of national governments to exert political control over their territories. The impact of globalization on conventional forms of territoriality and related changes to the international system also involve an important subset of topics. These include the proliferation and growing impact of nonstate actors in recent decades, the related emergence of a *global civil society* that is no longer confined within the borders of the territorial state, and the prospects for new *global governance structures* understood as the norms and institutions that define and mediate relations between citizens, societies, markets, and states on a global scale. In short, the concepts of *territoriality* and *sovereignty* sit at the very core of political domain theories of globalization.

Territoriality refers to both the condition of demarcated political space and the use of territory for political, social, and economic ends. In the discourses of Western modernity, the term has been associated with a largely successful strategy for establishing the exclusive jurisdiction implied by state sovereignty.[17] State control of bounded national terrain promises citizens living on the inside the benefits of relative security and unity in exchange for their exclusive loyalty and allegiance to the nation-state. By the second half of the twentieth century, social existence in such relatively fixed spatial containers had gone on for such a long time that it struck most people as the universal mode of communal life in the world.

As discussed in the introduction, people developed a national imaginary, which naturalized ideas and feelings of belonging to the nation-state. However, the wave of neoliberal economic globalization in the 1990s unsettled this normalized political template. The intensifying twin dynamics of *denationalization* and *deterritorialization* boosted by turbocapitalism and digital technology exposed the artificiality of national territoriality. The rising global imaginary also unsettled the theoretical status of the nation-state as a social construct and exposed its historical role as a specific human technique for managing political space in the interest of modern state power. As noted, this theoretical unsettlement penetrated deeply into the academic template of IR theory and its associated methodological nationalism, which considered nation-states as the principal actors on the world stage. Challenging IR theory, globalization theorists instead embraced a methodological globalism, which adopted transnational or *deterritorialized* connections and flows as its basic units of analysis.

We might refer to the group of domain thinkers who take the process of deterritorialization to the extreme as *deterritorial absolutists*. This approach to analyzing political space rose to prominence during the 1990s when spectacular neoliberal market reforms appeared to permanently diminish the role of the state in the economy. Neoliberal thinkers like the prominent Japanese management expert Kenichi Ohmae embrace deterritorialization as the precondition for the creation of an ultracompetitive borderless world.[18] They suggest that political space anchored in conventional territoriality is losing out to an unstoppable techno-economic juggernaut, which crushes national forms of sovereignty understood as the state's exclusive control of strict and fixed territorial boundaries. In addition, deterritorial absolutists

86 / Domain Theories

emphasize that states are less able to determine the direction of social life *within* their borders. Since the workings of global capital markets are erasing the distinction between inner and outer political space, territorially based states have become vulnerable to the discipline imposed by economic choices made elsewhere and over which they have no practical control. Hence, deterritorial absolutists predict that the role of government will ultimately be reduced to serving as a *superconductor for global capitalism*.[19] Indeed, their central message is loud and clear: the end of the nation-state is at hand.

However, this absolutist perspective is challenged by a group of more moderate political domain thinkers we may call *deterritorial relativists*. Their theoretical models point to the continued relevance of conventional political units, albeit in reconfigured forms. At the same time, deterritorial relativists realize that neoliberal economic globalization has significantly constrained the set of political options open to states, particularly in the Global South. Still, influential voices like the European globalization theorist Jan Aart Scholte assert that political globalization involves at its core significant spatial processes of deterritorialization reflected in the large-scale spread of *supraterritoriality*. This term refers to networks of interconnectivity that substantially transcend nation-state-based territorial geography. As Scholte explains, these connections possess spatiotemporal qualities of *transworld simultaneity*—extension anywhere across the planet at the same time—and *transworld instantaneity*—movement anywhere on the planet in no time.[20] Multiplying supraterritorial forms of globality are evident in countless facets of contemporary life such as jet travel across any distance on the planet in twenty-four hours or less, worldwide telecommunications networks, global financial flows, and so on.

Domain Theories / 87

> **Jan Aart Scholte (1959–)** is Professor of Global Transformations and Governance Challenges at Leiden University, Netherlands. His research covers globalization, global governance, civil society in global politics, global democracy, legitimacy in global governance, global Internet governance, and methodologies of global studies. Another of his long-term research concerns addresses democracy in global politics, often with a particular focus on the expanding role of civil society. His major contribution to globalization theory comes in the form of a sophisticated analysis of the workings of deterritorialization dynamics and their impact on conventional structures of political space such as nation-states as well as nonstate actors.

Moreover, Scholte notes that the principle of exclusive state sovereignty has been giving way to pooled or shared forms of sovereignty.[21] While these new arrangements increase the inability of nation-states to manage the globalization processes, they also force them to change into what some thinkers call a *network state*, characterized by shared sovereignty and responsibility, flexibility of procedures of governance, and greater diversity and flexibility in the relationships between governments and citizens.[22] While sharing some similarities with Robinson's TNS model, this conception of globalizing political spaces differs in that it puts less emphasis on class and social stratification. Moreover, Scholte rejects absolutist pronouncements of the demise of the nation-state by demonstrating that states are still capable of regulating social activities to a significant extent. Hence, they are far from being impotent bystanders to the workings of global economic forces.[23]

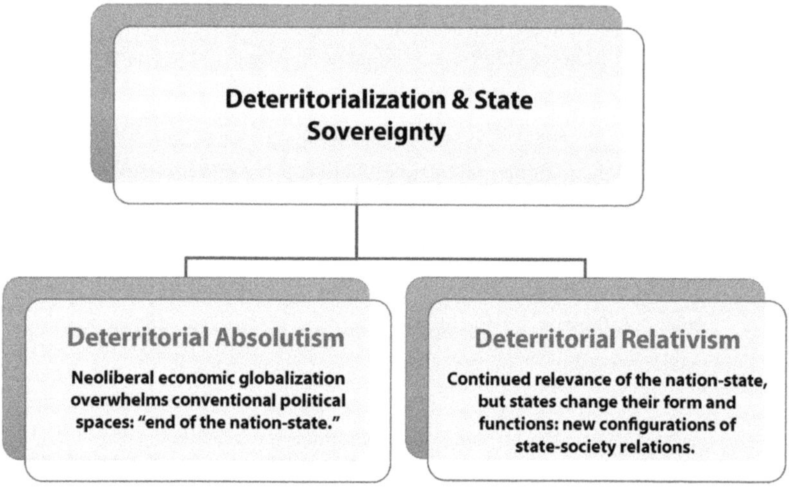

Deterritorialization & State Sovereignty

Deterritorial Absolutism

Neoliberal economic globalization overwhelms conventional political spaces: "end of the nation-state."

Deterritorial Relativism

Continued relevance of the nation-state, but states change their form and functions: new configurations of state-society relations.

Figure 9. Deterritorialization absolutists and relativists

Fellow deterritorial relativists like the American literary theorist Michael Hardt and the Italian political philosopher Antonio Negri concur with Scholte's thesis that the decline of nation-state sovereignty cannot be equated with the eclipse of sovereignty as such. However, their political domain thinking proceeds along different lines. Focusing on the rapidly transforming form and functions of sovereignty, they suggest that political globalization produces a new deterritorialized apparatus of political authority and control they call *Empire*. For Hardt and Negri, Empire is not merely a catchy metaphor but an entirely new global order composed of a series of national and supranational institutions that have succeeded conventional nation-state-centered forms of sovereignty.[24] This new regime neither establishes territorial centers nor relies on fixed boundaries. Rather it manages intensifying social interconnectivities through the establishment of global networks of command. No longer opposed by an extrasystemic outside, this new form of sovereignty constitutes a regime that effectively encompasses the spatial totality of the entire globe.

Although Hardt and Negri place stronger emphasis on the decline of national sovereignty than Scholte, they agree with their fellow political domain thinker that today's deterritorialization processes entail spatial reconfigurations of sovereignty that involve primarily a process of upscaling from the national to the global. Challenging neoliberal models of global capitalism, Hardt and Negri also suggest that globalization cannot be reduced to processes of economic deregulation, privatization, and trade liberalization, which will eventually lead to the demise of the nation-state-based international system. Rather, Empire wields sovereign power as *the* governing global political subject that reregulates *all* forms of social exchange. More than just an empire of capital, this global regime permeates all spheres of social life, including the creation of new technologies, the expansion of vast circuits of material and immaterial production, the movement of gigantic cultural flows, and the management of new hybrid identities.[25] At this point, Hardt and Negri's political perspective touches upon the cultural domain of globalization, to which we turn next.

HYBRIDIZING GLOBAL CULTURE

A number of prominent domain thinkers have suggested that globalization lies at the heart of modern culture, just as cultural practices lie at the heart of globalization.[26] After all, today's global cultural flows are directed by powerful international media corporations that utilize transnational communication technologies to shape societies and identities. As ideas and images can be transmitted more easily and quickly from one place to another, they profoundly impact the way people experience their everyday lives in their local environments. Consequently, deep-seated cultural understandings and practices often struggle to keep their roots in fixed localities such as town and nation. As intensifying waves of *cultural globalization* challenge and unsettle conventional ways of life, they might either harden traditional values and identities or infuse them with altered meanings that reflect incoming cultural symbols and discourses. Hence, it is not surprising that the related topic of *cultural difference* has dominated theoretical inquiries into cultural globalization: does globalization erase cultural differences and thereby breed cultural *homogeneity* (sameness), or does it encourage greater cultural *heterogeneity* (difference)?

Cultural domain thinkers usually preface their investigations of this central question by defining their key concept. Most of these designations center on the ways in which people make their lives meaningful by communicating with each other. In other words, "culture" is presented as the equivalent to general human software reflected in our capacity for language, using symbols and communicating meanings that enable us to navigate our complex social and natural environments. To be sure, such generic definitions of culture require finetuning insofar as meanings find their material expression only in concrete social settings and contexts. Cultural domain thinkers also tend to find common theoretical ground in their understanding of globalization as a set of social processes driving increasing worldwide interconnectivity.[27] Thus arriving at converging definitions of their two keywords, they nonetheless diverge when it comes to their assessments of the impact of globalization on cultural difference.

One group of thinkers argue that cultural globalization has facilitated the rise of a homogenized global culture underwritten by an Anglo-American value system. Referring to this worldwide diffusion of Western consumerism and lifestyles as *Americanization* or *westernization*, these authors theorize the ways in which such forms of *cultural imperialism* are overwhelming more vulnerable cultures.[28] This concept refers to the domination of one culture by another, which includes a spectrum of measures running from persuasion and bribery to open force.[29] Empirical evidence cited in support of the cultural imperialism thesis includes Amazonian Indians wearing Nike sneakers, denizens of the southern Sahara purchasing Texaco baseball caps, and Palestinian youths proudly displaying their Chicago Bulls sweatshirts in downtown Ramallah. Domain thinkers like the American political theorist Benjamin Barber refer to the dominant value system created by cultural globalization as *McWorld*. This term captures the power of a superficial American popular culture assembled in the 1950s and 1960s that is driven by expansionist commercial interests. As Barber observes, "Its [McWorld's] template is American, its form style ... music, video, theater, books, and theme parks ... are all constructed as image exports creating a common taste around common logos, advertising slogans, stars, songs, brand names, jingles, and trademarks."[30]

Homogenization thinkers like George Ritzer argue that cultural imperialism is also reflected in a worldwide standardization of lifestyles. The American sociologist coined the term *McDonaldization* to describe the wide-ranging process of rational standardization by which the principles of fast-food restaurants like McDonald's and KFC are coming to dominate the social organization of businesses in more and more regions of the world. On the surface, these principles appear to be rational in their attempts to offer efficient, predictable, and profitable ways of serving customers' material needs. However, such rational systems also tend to erase unique expressions of human creativity and cultural difference, which means that they contribute to the rise of irrationality in the world. In the long run, Ritzer predicts, McDonaldization does not merely spell the eclipse of cultural diversity, but also contributes to the dehumanization of *all* social relations.[31]

Some domain thinkers even go so far as to suggest that the consumerist push toward planetary uniformity in the image of the West will inevitably result in the wholesale imposition of the cultural order of the West and the destruction of diverse ways of life in other parts of the world. Critical proponents of the cultural sameness thesis attribute the alleged rise of the American-sponsored global monoculture to commodifying practices of neoliberal capitalism. TNCs, especially Big Tech and social media corporations, are often singled out as the main engines driving the creation of McWorld that regards all aspects of human life as things that can be bought and sold. Serving as the new missionaries of global capitalism, these corporate giants overwhelm the rest of the world with consumerist messages and images conveyed by their powerful digital networks and social media sites. The thesis of the spread of a capitalist monoculture also points to the influence of the Anglo-American culture industry to make English the global lingua franca of the twenty-first century.[32]

It is one thing to acknowledge the powerful cultural logic of global capitalism, but it is quite another to assert that the cultural differences existing on our planet are destined to vanish altogether. Accordingly, dissenting advocates of *cultural differentialism* argue in favor of enduring cultural essences. While acknowledging westernization as a major force that impacts people's ways of life, they theorize that Americanization will fail to penetrate into the cultural core of non-Western societies. In fact, they suggest that cultural differences might even become more pronounced and weaponized in response to the onslaught of cultural imperialism. Barber's account of cultural globalization, for example, emphasizes that McWorld's expansionism has provoked powerful forms of resistance like *jihad*. He uses this term in a much broader sense than its Islamic association with "belligerent struggle" to characterize all parochial impulses to oppose Western homogenization forces wherever they can be found. Often fueled by the furies of nationalism or religious fundamentalism, jihad represents a "rabid response to colonialism and imperialism and their economic children, capitalism and modernity." Locked into opposing valorizations of homogeneity, jihad and McWorld find themselves dialectically enmeshed in a bitter cultural struggle for popular allegiance.[33]

Samuel P. Huntington offers a similar version of cultural differentialism which involves seven or eight contemporary *civilizations*. The American political scientist uses this term to describe the broadest level of culture and cultural identity, which tends to be enduring and rooted in religious belief systems. Thus, civilizations differ greatly on their underlying values systems and overall outlooks on life. Anchored in incompatible and immutable cultural values and linked to large-scale political agents like states and empires, these moving civilizational tectonic plates generate periodic earthquakes in the form of large-scale geopolitical conflicts. Like Barber's catchy metaphor of *McWorld versus jihad*, Huntington's influential thesis of a *clash of civilizations* singles out the current struggle between the Judeo-Christian West based on "universalist values" and an Islamic East attached to forms of cultural "particularism."[34]

94 / *Domain Theories*

Both domain thinkers embrace what could be called a *billiard ball model of culture* consisting of separate and impenetrable units that can only be understood from within and on their own terms. Pushed hard by the intensifying forces of globalization, these billiard balls can easily become weaponized projectiles in the hands of political actors who aim to inflict the greatest possible damage on the "enemy." Hence, Huntington and Barber portray violent political conflict based on immutable cultural differences as a perennial feature of human history. The lesson to be learned by the West—and the "rest"—is not the art of initiating cross-cultural dialogue, but the best way of strengthening their own cultural core values in order to prevail in the clash of civilizations. As might be expected, such binary accounts of cultural difference received special attention in the wake of the al-Qaeda terrorist attacks of September 11, 2001.

Firmly opposed to the differentialist image of culture as fixed pieces tied to locality and tradition, Jan Nederveen Pieterse reads cultural globalization as resonating with a deterritorialized notion of culture as fluid, open-ended, and, most importantly, *mixed*. At the same time, the Dutch global studies scholar also rejects cultural sameness theories as geographically narrow and historically shallow. In his view, these two dominant responses to the question of cultural difference miss an important third alternative, which seems to become ever more prominent under conditions of growing worldwide interdependence: *hybridization*.

Signifying the mixture of different elements and strands, hybridity is a multipurpose concept that describes such different things as designer agricultural seeds, cars running on dual combustion and electric engines, companies that blend American and Japanese management practices, multiracial people, dual

> **Jan Nederveen Pieterse (1946–)** is the Duncan and Suzanne Mellichamp Distinguished Professor of Global Studies at the University of California, Santa Barbara. Besides maintaining a strong focus on cultural globalization, Pieterse's numerous publications cover the fields of social anthropology, global political economy, and development studies. His most important contribution to globalization theory is his conceptualization of cultural globalization as hybridization that gives rise to a global mélange. In his later writings, Pieterse expands his cultural focus, arguing that hybridization processes also apply to wider structural forms of social life, including nation-state formation, urbanization, international law, and modes of economic production.

citizens, artificial languages like Esperanto, and cross-bred animals.[35] As Pieterse explains,

> Hybridity goes under various aliases such as syncretism, creolization, métissage, mestizaje, crossover.... Hybridization may conceal the asymmetry and unevenness in the process and the elements of mixing. Distinctions need to be made between different times, patterns, types, and styles of mixing; besides, mixing carries different meanings in different cultural contexts.[36]

Applying hybridization processes to cultural globalization dynamics, Pieterse highlights the intermingling of cultures and identities from different territorial locations. The increasing traffic between cultures across the planet has created new zones of hybridization where meanings derive from different historical sources that were originally separated from one another in space but have come to mingle extensively. Given the unsettling of culture and place, Pieterse suggests that cultural globalization should be seen as the hybridization of symbolic forms and identities that gives rise to a *global mélange*.[37] As globalization intensifies, such manifestations of cultural mixing are increasingly visible in music, film, fashion, language, and other forms of symbolic expression. Pieterse mentions concrete examples of global mixtures of cultural phenomena that are generally held to be incongruent, such as Thai boxing by Moroccan girls in Amsterdam, Asian rap in London, Irish bagels sold on the streets of Sydney, Chinese and Korean tacos, Mexican schoolgirls dressed in Greek togas dancing in the style of Isadora Duncan, Japanese Kabuki actors performing a Shakespeare play for a Paris audience, and a Greek restaurant called Ipanema serving Italian food in Brighton.[38]

Rather than being obliterated by Western consumerist forces of homogenization, local difference and particularity also encourage the formation of hybrid translocal identities. Such identities might encompass several nationalities, combine different racial and ethnic categories, associate with multifaceted forms of sexuality, or combine different class contexts.[39] Pieterse concedes that applying a hybridity lens to globalization processes does not rule out the possibility of cultural struggles. Still, a multifocused view on conflict involving hybrid forms opens the door to theories contesting the antagonistic "us versus them" dichotomy that defines the two dominant perspectives on cultural difference. For this reason, Pieterse's hybridization approach to cultural globalization does not merely challenge binary thinking on cultural matters, but it also defies pernicious doctrines of racial purity that condemn all practices of "mixing," especially in the form of human "half-breeds."

Combining his domain approach with the critical mode of thinking elaborated in chapter 4, Pieterse suggests that hybridization can be an empowering perspective that serves as a critique of all forms of cultural essentialism that underlie romantic nationalism, racism, religious revivalism, and civilizational chauvinism.[40] Used in this way, hybridity turns from a pejorative term to an emancipatory concept that can serve as an analytical tool for exposing asymmetrical power relations. It allows theorists to connect the empirical world—the social arenas where hybridization happens—with normative thinking that questions the valorization of socially constructed boundaries linked to the habitual denigration of mixtures.

Such critical styles of hybridity thinking seem to be especially promising when applied to global migration issues. Rather than seeing the immigration of outsiders into one's homeland through the exclusivist lenses of cultural differentialism, the hybridization paradigm suggests that both aliens and national citizens embody mixed cultural traits. Acknowledging hybridity all the way down as the norm rather than the exception encourages the design of integrative migration policies that accept and accommodate cultural differences without essentializing them. Moreover, the recognition of our fundamental human condition as both mixed and mixable translates more easily into a celebration of cultural diversity. Accordingly, hybridization thinkers of the cultural domain have welcomed the compression of world-space and world-time as the catalyst for the creation of new expressions of cultural diversity.[41] By showing how global cultural flows often reinvigorate local cultural niches, they emphasize that globalization always takes place in local contexts. Such processes drive the pluralization of the world insofar as local expressions are reflected on the global level and vice versa. Hence, the dynamic of cultural globalization can be adequately captured neither by the notion of growing sameness nor by the idea of enduring

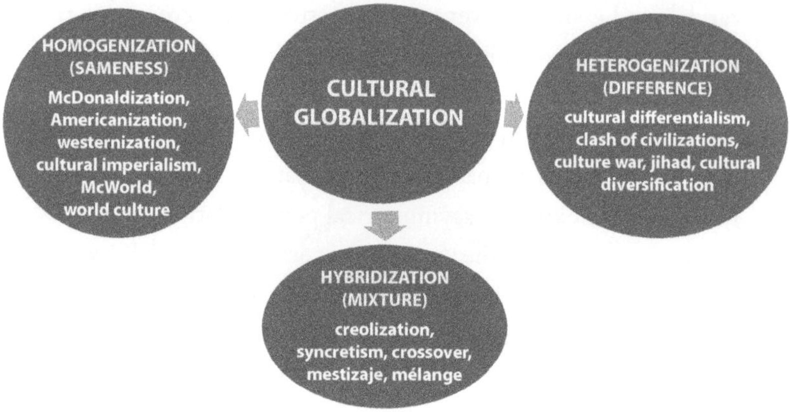

Figure 10. Three theories of cultural globalization

cultural differences, but by the vision of *glocalization*—the interaction of the global and the local characterized by cultural borrowing and mixing.[42]

CONCLUDING CRITICAL REFLECTIONS

There are clear upsides to the domain mode of theorizing globalization. First, it encourages a more gradual approach to the subject by slicing it up into more digestible chunks.

Second, it makes for deeper understandings of major globalization dimensions, each of which can be further disaggregated into smaller components and processes. Unlike general theorists who seek to identify comprehensive patterns of globalization at the macro level, domain theorists construct their analytic models on a lower level of abstraction linked to specific areas or dimensions of global interconnectivity and mobility. Such midrange analyses give domain theories more precision and focus. Indeed, the primary objective of domain theorizing is quite moderate and thus more achievable in its aim to generate *partial insights* and claims of limited *range and applicability.*

Third, domain thinking allows for the recombination of single globalization aspects into multidimensional models. These can be assembled collaboratively in multidisciplinary projects that cut across the social sciences and humanities.

Fourth, domain thinkers are steeped in the scope and methods of their academic disciplines, which allows them to apply their specific expertise quickly and efficiently to the study of globalization.

Fifth, the domain mode of theorizing globalization often produces what might be called an *add-on effect.* Once major dimensions have been mapped and analyzed in some detail, it becomes easier to outline and explore more domains. In other words, existing domain knowledge facilitates the open-ended addition of new dimensions. As we noted in this chapter, the original confinement of globalization theory to only three or four dimensions was rapidly overcome by the contributions of scholars new to globalization research.

On the flipside, however, each of these virtues of domain thinking also harbors potential shortcomings. On the first point, the advantage of entering the arena of globalization theory gradually by focusing on a single dimension is undercut by the temptation to remain there. As theorists become more comfortable with a specific domain, they are more likely to deepen their analysis in their familiar area rather than risking the difficult shift to another domain. In short, shining the theoretical spotlight on a single aspect of globalization heightens the danger of one-dimensional thinking. It appears that one way around this problem is related to the third point, namely, to combine partial insights by means of multidisciplinary collaborations. Yet, such a collective operation might not go far enough. While multidisciplinarity constitutes a big step forward, it nonetheless struggles to facilitate deep levels of integration that are necessary for assembling a sharper multidimensional picture of globalization. We will return to this problem below.

Regarding the second point, the disaggregation of globalization into small components might yield richer insights into the intricacies of the chosen domain, but it also risks losing contact with the bigger picture. For example, Gary Gereffi's discerning theorizations of GVCs allow researchers to zoom in on important supply processes at the micro level, yet he rarely relates these findings back to the larger arena of economic globalization. In addition, Gereffi's analytical disaggregation expertly draws on empirical materials extracted from large data sets, but neglects the equally important task of normative reflection and theory building.

On the third and fourth point, let us note that laudable efforts to assemble multidimensional models of globalization through multidisciplinary collaborations among discipline-based scholars face two distinct problems. For one, it is immensely difficult to fuse specific insights into a bigger picture without lapsing into the generalizing mode of creating a macro-analytic framework. For example, Robinson's domain mode of theorizing global capitalism starts in the economic world of the TNCs, but soon branches out into the political realm to capture the related phenomena of the TCC and the TNS. His understandable desire to grasp the full dynamics of global capitalism pushes him into a macro-theoretical framework whose grand narrative is too abstract to appeal to most readers. Moreover, Robinson's analytical upshifting flirts with a built-in Eurocentrism that measures capitalism in relation to Western modernity and its supposedly "universal" standards. Rather than recognizing the great variety of capitalisms that exist in the world today, Robinson's embrace of general thinking reduces "global capitalism" to a single, universal category of Western parentage.

The other drawback linked to assembling multidimensional models of globalization through multidisciplinary collaborations is that these operations fall short of full transdisciplinary integration. Let us consider this problem in more detail. Derived from the Latin word *multus* ("many"), the concept of *multidisciplinarity* refers to activities drawing on knowledge from different disciplines that involve tight coordination among disciplines without achieving deep integration. Hence it makes sense to liken multidisciplinarity to "a bowl of fruit containing a variety of fruits, each fruit representing a discipline and being in close proximity to the others."[43] In most cases, members from different disciplines come together around a particular project that would benefit from a variety of methodological approaches. Still, multidisciplinarians work independently on different aspects of their common project—often in a parallel or sequential manner. Proceeding in a self-contained fashion, they stay largely within their own disciplinary boundaries and require only few opportunities for intercommunication. The resulting lack of integration, however, prevents multidisciplinary projects to make even richer contributions to our knowledge of globalization. Rather than learning *from* each other, multidisciplinarians learn more *about* each other's separate modes of theorizing globalization. The ultimate outcome of multidisciplinary efforts is merely cumulative, that is, the sum of the individual parts.

The concept of *transdisciplinarity* is configured around the Latin prefix *trans* ("across" or "beyond"). It signifies the systemic and holistic integration of diverse forms of knowledge by cutting *across* and through existing disciplinary boundaries and paradigms in ways that reach *beyond* each individual discipline. Thus, transdisciplinarity offers a deep fusion of disciplinary knowledge that produces new understandings capable of transforming or restructuring existing knowledge paradigms. Still, the transdisciplinary imperative to challenge, go beyond, transgress, and unify separate orientations does not ignore the importance of attracting scholars with specific disciplinary backgrounds. Rather, transdisciplinary teams often work by using a shared conceptual framework, drawing together discipline-specific theories, concepts, and approaches to address the larger phenomenon.[44] Rather than just assembling multidimensional models of globalization through multidisciplinary collaborations, transdisciplinarians aim at a deep integration—even fusion—of disciplinary knowledge. And it is this very goal of transdisciplinary fusion that seems to be incompatible with a cumulative domain style of thinking.

Finally, regarding the fifth point of the adding of extra dimensions of globalization might, indeed, heighten our recognition of the immensity of space-time compression. Yet, it also multiplies disagreements over which of these domains should be considered more significant than others. For example, is military globalization more important than ideological globalization? Should theories of gender globalization be given precedence over explorations of the growing interconnectivities in the art world? Since it is unlikely that these aspects are all equally important, the problem becomes one of weighing and then assigning priority to one domain over another. In the end, it is unlikely that such complicated procedures will result in widespread academic agreement. While a certain amount of disagreement is necessary for the advancement of knowledge, too much of it results in a cacophony of voices, each of which clamors for the primary importance of its own domain. Nonetheless, in spite of inviting confusion, the open-ended addition of domains also offers a final advantage of domain thinking: it brings into sharper focus the mind-boggling complexity of globalization.

As some globalization scholars recognize, the increasing complexity of our interconnected world requires a distinct mode of theorizing, which will be discussed in the next chapter.

NOTES

1. Robert K. Merton, *Social Theory and Social Structure* (New York: Free Press, 1968).

2. See the book series edited by Manfred B. Steger and Terrell Carver with Rowman & Littlefield: https://rowman.com/Action /SERIES/_/GLO/Globalization#; and the book series edited by Barry Gills with Routledge: www.routledge.com/Rethinking-Globalizations/book-series/RG.

3. Robert Gilpin, *The Challenge of Global Capitalism: The World Economy in the 21st Century*, 3rd ed. (Princeton, NJ: Princeton University Press, 2002).

4. Peter Dicken, *Global Shift: Mapping the Changing Contours of the World Economy*, 6th ed. (New York: Guilford Press, 2011).

5. Manfred B. Steger and Ravi Roy, *Neoliberalism: A Very Short Introduction*, 2nd ed. (Oxford, UK: Oxford University Press, 2021).

6. Theodore Levitt, "The Globalization of Markets," *Harvard Business Review* 61, no. 3 (1983): 92–102.

7. Thomas L. Friedman, *The Lexus and the Olive Tree: Understanding Globalization* (New York: Random House, 2000), ix–xii, xxi, 8–9, 27.

8. Immanuel Wallerstein, *World-Systems Analysis: An Introduction* (Durham, NC: Duke University Press, 2004).

9. Wallerstein, x.

10. William I. Robinson and Federico Fuentes, "Capitalist Globalisation, Transnational Class Exploitation and the Global Police State: An Interview with William I. Robinson," *Anti-Capitalist Resistance*, October 19, 2023, https://anticapitalistresistance.org/capitalist-globalisation-

transnational-class-exploitation-and-the-global-police-state-an-interview-with-william-i-robinson/.

11. William I. Robinson, *A Theory of Global Capitalism: Production, Class, and State in a Transnational World* (Baltimore: Johns Hopkins University Press, 2004), 11.

12. Robinson, 14.

13. Gary Gereffi and Katrina Fernandez-Stark, *Global Value Chains: A Primer*, Duke Center on Globalization, Governance & Competitiveness at the Social Science Research Institute, July 2016, https://dukespace.lib.duke.edu/server/api/core/bitstreams/fd7a47de-df3b-4a75-9749-e5113e28def3/content; Dicken, *Global Shift*.

14. William I. Robinson, "Global Capitalism: Reflections on a Brave New World," *Great Transition Initiative*, June 2017, www.tellus.org/pub/Robinson-Global-Capitalism_1.pdf.

15. Robinson, *Theory of Global Capitalism*, 21.

16. Robinson, "Global Capitalism," 11. See also, Robinson, *Global Capitalism and the Crisis of Humanity* (Cambridge, UK: Cambridge University Press, 2014); and Robinson, *Global Civil War: Capitalism Post-Pandemic* (Oakland, CA: PM Press, 2022).

17. John Agnew, *Globalization & Sovereignty* (Lanham, MD: Rowman & Littlefield, 2009), 6.

18. Kenichi Ohmae, *The Borderless World: Power and Strategy in the Interlinked World Economy* (New York: Harper Business, 1990); Kenichi Ohmae, *The End of the Nation-State: The Rise of Regional Economies* (New York: Free Press, 1995).

19. Lowell Bryan and Diana Farrell, *Market Unbound: Unleashing Global Capitalism* (New York: John Wiley & Sons, 1996), 187.

20. Jan Aart Scholte, *Globalization: A Critical Introduction*, 2nd ed. (New York: St. Martin's Press, 2005), 61.

21. Scholte, 190–91.

22. Manuel Castells, "The New Public Sphere: Global Civil Society, Communication Networks, and Global Governance," *Annals of the American Academy of Political and Social Science* 616, no. 1 (2008): 88.

23. Scholte, *Globalization*, 77.

24. Michael Hardt and Antonio Negri, *Empire* (Cambridge, MA: Harvard University Press, 2000), 353, 413.

25. Hardt and Negri, xi–xvi.

26. John Tomlinson, *Globalization and Culture* (Chicago: University of Chicago Press, 1999), 1.

27. Tomlinson, 2, 18; Jan Nederveen Pieterse, *Globalization and Culture: Global Mélange*, 4th ed. (Lanham, MD: Rowman & Littlefield, 2020), 18, 33.

28. Serge Latouche, *The Westernization of the World* (Cambridge: Polity Press, 1996), 3.

29. Herbert Schiller, *Communication and Cultural Domination* (Armonk, NY: International Arts and Sciences Press, 1976), 9.

30. Benjamin R. Barber, *Jihad vs. McWorld* (New York: Ballantine Books, 1996), 17.

31. George Ritzer, *The McDonaldization of Society: An Investigation into the Changing Character of Contemporary Social Life* (Thousand Oaks, CA: Pine Forge Press, 1993).

32. Robert McCrum, *Globish: How English Became the World's Language* (New York: W.W. Norton, 2011).

33. Barber, *Jihad vs. McWorld*, 19.

34. Samuel P. Huntington, *The Clash of Civilizations and the Remaking of World Order* (New York: Touchstone, 1997).

35. Marwan M. Kraidy, *Hybridity: Or the Cultural Logic of Globalization* (Philadelphia: Temple University Press, 2005), 1.

36. Pieterse, *Globalization and Culture*, 71.

37. Pieterse, 5.

38. Pieterse, 91, 138.

39. Scholte, *Globalization*, 252.

40. Pieterse, *Globalization and Culture*, 105.

41. Robertson, *Globalization*; Ulf Hannerz, *Transnational Connections: Cultures, People, Places* (London: Routledge, 1996).

42. Victor Roudometof, *Glocalization: A Critical Introduction* (London: Routledge, 2016).

43. Allen F. Repko, *Interdisciplinary Research: Process and Theory*, 2nd ed. (London: Sage, 2011), 17.

44. Bernard C.K. Choi and Anita W.P. Pak, "Multidisciplinarity, Interdisciplinarity, and Transdisciplinarity in Health Research, Education and Policy: Definitions, Objectives, and Evidence of Effectiveness," *Clinical and Investigative Medicine* 29, no. 6 (2006): 355.

CHAPTER THREE

Complexity Theories

This chapter provides an overview of influential theories of globalization composed in the complexity style of inquiry. After a brief explanation of complexity theory and its primary features, we explore this mode of theorizing globalization by turning to the works of three prominent thinkers.

We start with Saskia Sassen's innovative attempt to understand shifting spatial arrangements created by globalization. Emphasizing the centrality of *urban spaces* for key transnational economic actors like large financial and service firms, the Dutch sociologist argues that globalization does not just happen on the global level, but engages all spatial scales at the same time. For Sassen, theorizing globalization dynamics in *global cities* and other *glocal contexts* is also meant to set an example for other scholars to pay greater attention to the spatial intersections of our globalizing world.

Next, we consider the influential globalization theory of Manuel Castells. The Spanish social thinker utilizes the com-

Complexity Theories / 107

plexity mode to analyze the workings of what he calls the *global network society* anchored in the sprawling webs of digital information and communication. His empirically grounded investigation of these global social and organizational interdependencies is especially oriented to the new economy of digital capitalism, which has been rapidly replacing established economic practices based on centralized business structures and hierarchical management.

This discussion of the rise of networked global formations is followed by a consideration of John Urry's exploration of what he sees as the liquid character of contemporary social relations. For the British thinker, the key to examining globalization lies in the *globally integrated networks* and *global fluids*, which form complex and often contradictory relationships with each other. While sharing Castells's penchant for the complexity style of theorizing, Urry argues that the latter's "network" metaphor does not do full justice to the intricate dynamics that go by the name of "globalization." To remedy the perceived shortcoming of network theory, Urry introduces a new vocabulary into globalization theory, which forms the conceptual backbone of his transdisciplinary analysis of global complexity.

All of the theorists discussed in this chapter emphasize that social theory should no longer be focused on nationally bounded societies. Hence, they share a special affinity for a *methodological glocalism*, which is extremely compatible with the complexity approach to globalization. At the same time, however, they combine their primary mode of theorizing with some of the other styles of thinking presented in this book. The chapter ends with a critical evaluation of some major strengths and weaknesses of the complexity mode of theorizing globalization.

THE COMPLEXITY MODE OF THEORIZING

There exists a rare consensus among globalization theorists that the compression of world-space and world-time involves the creation and development of *complex* and *uneven* webs of global interconnectivity and mobility. *Complexity* refers to multiple and intricate contacts among a large number of related elements and dynamics that often result in unanticipated outcomes. Early scientific usages of this concept outside of its colloquial equivalents "complicated" and "messy" have occurred in the fields of cybernetics, computer science, mathematics, psychology, and the natural sciences, particularly in physics, chemistry, and biology. As we noted in chapter 1, Einstein and other pioneers of quantum physics argued that time and space are neither static nor objective categories, but *internal* to the very processes by which our physical and social worlds operate. Such a relativist perspective supports the thesis that time and space are not fixed categories but variable dimensions. In other words, these basic dimensions that frame our existence are far from static, but appear to "flow." As the prominent British physicist Stephen Hawking puts it, "Space and time are now dynamic qualities: when a body moves, or a force acts, it affects the curvature of space and time—and in turn the structure of space-time affects the way in which bodies move and forces act."[1]

Quantum theorists characterize the behavior of subatomic particles as *relational* also in the sense that gaining an understanding of their complex interactions is more fundamental than ascertaining their status as individual elements. This means that the smallest particles of matter have no standing as isolated entities, but should be conceptualized as a complex assemblage, which is also connected to external processes of observation and meas-

Complexity Theories / 109

urement. Such fundamental relationality of all matter also means that things exist only *contingently* by depending on other things. The Anglo-American physicist David Bohm aptly refers to these subtle and dynamic webs of complex interdependence that govern our universe as "a dance without dancers."[2]

By contrast, traditional science prioritizes the investigation of linear cause-effect relationships. As we discussed previously, insights are gained through various reductionistic frameworks that disaggregate the considered entity into its constituent parts. Understanding the workings of the smaller parts is treated by conventional science as an indispensable precondition for gaining a better grasp of the larger phenomenon.

Complexity theorists find this mechanistic framework too static and limiting. They turn their analytical spotlight instead to interactive, open-ended dynamics that give rise to ever new formations. This means that they consider the whole as qualitatively greater—and often quite different from—the sum of its parts. Moreover, complexity theorists resist the conventional scientific division of phenomena into purified sets belonging to either the natural or the social sciences. Arguing that both knowledge domains are subject to complex processes, they emphasize instead multiple convergences, overlaps, and interdependencies that connect these realms. This strong emphasis on boundary-crossing interactions rather than self-enclosed binaries is reflected in the complexity worldview of the German quantum physicist Werner Heisenberg: "The world thus appears as a complicated tissue of events, in which connections of different kinds alternate or overlap or combine and thereby determine the texture of the whole."[3]

The complexity mode of inquiry has been connected to *systems theory*. Pioneered by early twentieth-century biologists, it originally applied to the study of living organisms in their natural habitats as integrated wholes. A *system* is an interactive set of elements that can be differentiated from other dynamics that occur outside its stated limits. Although the drawing of such lines of demarcation can be especially difficult in the case of social systems, complexity thinkers argue it is possible to model distinct structures and substructures—even if we acknowledge that system boundaries are never entirely closed to external influences.

Systems theory also sharpens researchers' ability to shift between different levels of analysis, including the micro-behavior of component parts and the structural dynamics on the macro level. Multilevel systems such as ecosystems, global communication networks, and urban infrastructures are characterized as *complex adaptive systems* (CAS).[4] They are capable of reordering their structural configurations through the exchange of new information, energy, and other resources within their natural and social environments. This means that all systems rely on positive feedback loops, which make it easier for them to adapt to their ever-changing environment. In fact, they develop "emergent properties" that evolve into new states and configurations. For this reason, *responsive, emergent, spontaneous,* and *unpredictable* are crucial concepts in the analytic arsenal of complexity theory.

To sum up, then, complexity thinking investigates the emergent, dynamic, self-organizing, and interdependent dynamics of natural and social systems that interact with each other in ways that influence and shape existing configurations.[5] Since the 1980s, academic research into various forms and systems of complexity has been conducted in pioneering centers like the Santa Fe Institute in New Mexico. The stated mission of such innovative institutes is to expand our knowledge of patterns and proc-

Figure 11. Attributes of complexity theory

esses of complexity manifested in our physical, biological, social, cultural, technological, and astrobiological worlds.[6]

Following the lead of their colleagues in the natural sciences, globalization theorists writing in the complexity mode approach globalization as an intricate, interactive, and highly contingent phenomenon. The primary goals of their complexity thinking are to analyze the many conditions of complex global connectivity and then to interpret their implications across various spheres of social life. Thus, complexity theorists present the evolving condition of globality as a self-organizing system, which both produces and is being produced by overlapping and open-ended interdependencies. Such a perspective eschews conventional social science frameworks that prioritize predictability and causality in favor of the production of sophisticated models of emergent interconnectivities and mobilities. Since global complexity appears in many forms and pervades all social arenas, theorists approach globalization from different angles

112 / *Complexity Theories*

and through multiple levels of analysis. As we shall see, their research efforts often involve empirical mappings of global configurations, which are articulated in the new complexity idiom of *networks, flows, fluids,* and *hybrids.*

Let us, then, examine the complexity mode of theorizing globalization in more detail through the works of three influential thinkers.

RESCALING GLOBALIZATION

As our discussion of deterritorialization in chapter 2 has shown, globalization dynamics are especially manifest in the complexity of spatial integration and differentiation. The *global village* is one of the most recognized and enduring phrases that reflect the growing public awareness of the power of interpenetrating spatial scales in our globalizing world. Coined by Marshall McLuhan in the early 1960s, the term captures the complex dynamics of spatial stretching that have made geographic distance much less of an obstacle in human interaction. As the Canadian media scholar observes, "After more than a century of electric technology, we have extended our central nervous system in a global embrace, abolishing both space and time as far as our planet is concerned."[7] Related concepts that affirm the significance of complex spatial compressions at the heart of globalization include: the *implosion of space*; *subduing space*; the *unreality of place*; the *shrinkage of space*; the *spatialization of time*; the *annihilation of space*; and *cyberspace*.[8]

To be sure, geographers and other space-orientated social thinkers have long emphasized the active role of space in structuring and reconfiguring human relations. In particular, they have pointed to the growing significance of the highest rung on the conventional spatial ladder extending from the local to the

Complexity Theories / 113

global. As the French philosopher Henri Lefebvre notes, "The creation (or production) of a *planet-wide* space as the social foundation of a transformed everyday life open to myriad possibilities—such is the dawn now beginning to break on the far horizon."[9]

However, such deserved attention to what appears to be explicitly global in scale does not mean that local, national, and regional levels have become less relevant in the global age. Quite to the contrary, globalization processes create incessantly new geographies and complex spatial arrangements from within subglobal spaces and places. Exploring the production of such novel spatialities in the global age, Saskia Sassen's writings are a lucid example of how the complexity mode of theorizing globalization can illuminate shifting spatial dynamics.

For Sassen, globalization involves two distinct dynamics, which conventional wisdom assigns to two different spatial scales. The *global scale* applies to the formation of explicitly *global* institutions and processes such as the UN, the WTO, financial markets, international war crimes tribunals, and so on. The second set of globalization processes does not necessarily scale at the global level, but is far more localized in *subglobal* settings such as nation-states, cities, and social institutions. These formations include, for example, cross-border networks of Latin American social activists engaged in specific localized struggles with an explicit global political agenda. Sassen suggests that, although such subglobal formations and processes shape events at the global scale in significant ways, they are usually not recognized as global.[10]

Applying the complexity mode of thinking in terms of emergent interdependencies rather than fixed spatial categories, Sassen contests watertight distinctions between global and local

Saskia Sassen (1947–) is Professor of Sociology and cochair of the Committee on Global Thought at Columbia University, USA. Her research interests include globalization theory, urban sociology, economic inequality, gender, and transnational migration. Sassen's pathbreaking analysis of global cities explains their pivotal role as command-and-control centers for the global economy as well as their increasing capacity to form strategic transnational networks. Thus, she shows how globalization processes reconfigure the capacity of cities, states, and institutional actors to shape global social connectivities. Sassen's globalization theory is consistently framed as the complex reorganization of territories, authority, and rights into new glocal assemblages.

levels. Rather, she asserts that the proliferation of complex sub-global dynamics as a result of globalization has led to a destabilization of familiar spatial hierarchies nested in vertical fashion at the local, national, regional, and global level. In other words, all social practices in today's world—economic, political, and cultural—are being affected by the increasing interpenetration of spatial scales. As Sassen summarizes, "Studying the global, then, entails a focus not only on that which is explicitly global in scale but also on locally scaled practices and conditions that are articulated with global dynamics."[11]

This destabilization of familiar *vertical* spatial hierarchies also means that the conventional vocabularies for describing nested geographic scales no longer provide adequate analytical tools for conceptualizing the *multiscalar* and interconnected character of contemporary globalization. Hence, Sassen urges globalization scholars to pay more attention to pertinent dynamics unfolding at subglobal scales and treat them for what they really are: crucial arenas of globalization processes. Sassen's recognition of the complexity of shifting geographic space allows her to provide a new conceptual language that allows for the rescaling of globalization from fixed vertical schemes to complex horizontal models. Constructs such as the *global city* and the *global-city region* are the key elements in her new conceptual architecture.[12]

Indeed, Sassen's most influential contribution to globalization theory concerns one of the most significant of these spatial restructuring processes in global cities such as New York, Paris, London, Tokyo, Shanghai, Seoul, Taipei, Mexico City, Mumbai, and Sydney. Of particular importance is the localization of the control and command centers of the main corporate actors of global capitalism. Globalizing economic networks rely more and more on the execution of the top-level financial, legal, managerial, and planning tasks necessary for the functioning of global corporations, especially in the finance and service sectors.

Sassen's complexity thinking shares much in common with David Harvey's *theory of* the *spatial fix*. The British geographer and global studies scholar first employed this term to describe capitalism's insatiable drive to resolve its crisis tendencies through the complex dynamics of geographical expansion and restructuring. Like Sassen, Harvey argues that capitalism's continuous attempts to fix spatial arrangements aspire to make them more favorable to its accumulation imperative. Such fixing occurs on all spatial scales ranging from, for example, the creation of local sweatshops in Mexico to the supranational integration of China in the WTO. As Harvey observes, "Capital is always in motion and much of that motion is spatial; commodity exchange ... always entails change of location and spatial movement. The market is spatialized ... and how that spatiality works has consequences for uneven geographical movement."[13]

On the surface, it looks like both Sassen and Harvey rely on the domain style of theorizing to gain new insights into the workings of global capitalism. After all, Sassen's central research question is about the pivotal role of global cities in the organization and management of the world economy. However, as Sassen continues to assemble what she calls the *global cities model*, it becomes clear that her analytic focus is even more on the *spatial complexities* involved in the activities of large economic firms headquartered in global cities. Although most of these megacities have longed served as international economic and cultural centers, processes of respatialization have become more complex and produced massive changes in their economic base and social structure. These massive transformations have impacted all spatial scales. For this reason, Sassen asserts that investigations of global cities should assume greater significance in globalization theory. They are pivotal places of complex spatial dispersals and global integrations located at the intersection of multiple global circuits and flows involving not just commodities and money, but also migrants, ideas, organizations, and cultural expressions.[14]

Moreover, Sassen proposes that global cities should be studied not as tightly bounded units, but as complex urban assemblages with vast hinterlands that are capable of reconstituting transnational economic processes as urban activities. While global cities remain encased in national territories, they are increasingly linked to other urban centers around the world. Hence, Sassen affirms that the glocalization of spaces plays important roles in the globalization process. What has traditionally

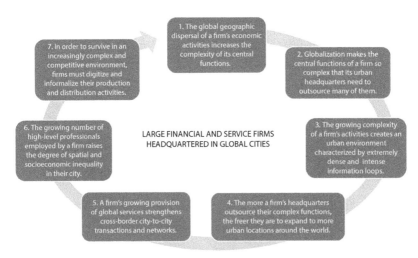

Figure 12. Saskia Sassen's global cities model: Seven complexity hypotheses

functioned—and been subjectively experienced—as national or local has been shifting away to more hybrid spatial manifestations. As Sassen notes, "Today we are seeing a partial unbundling of national space and the traditional hierarchies of scale centered on the national, with the city nested somewhere between the local and the region. This unbundling, even if partial, makes conceptualizing the city as nested in such hierarchies problematic."[15]

Overall, then, global cities serve as crucial catalysts for the formation of new transboundary spatialities required by the global economy. As place-based global networks, they owe much of their growing stature to the neoliberal economic policies of the 1990s that drove processes of deterritorialization. But the complex spatial dynamics of evolving globality not only result in the collapse of vertical geographic scales, but also lead to what Sassen calls *systemic expulsions*. These forced socioeconomic and environmental dislocations affect people, enterprises, and millions of animal and plant species and involve global complexities that cannot be fully understood through the linear cause-and-effect models of mainstream social science.[16]

Sassen's complexity style of thinking demonstrates that analyzing the shifting spatialities of our globalizing world leads to the construction of new theoretical models that can easily be extended beyond the narrow domain of economics. Globalization processes of all sorts unfold simultaneously in *all* dimensions and at *all* spatial scales. Consider, for example, Syrian migrants trying to reach Germany with the help of information gained from global digital devices. At the same time, they rely on locally organized, transnational human trafficking networks that rake in billions of untaxed "service" dollars in the process. To a significant extent, then, getting a better grasp of such intricate glocal dynamics occurring in all social domains depends on the ability of thinkers like Saskia Sassen to utilize the complexity style of theorizing.

NETWORKING GLOBALIZATION

As globalization theory began to flourish at the turn of the twenty-first century, scholars increasingly seized upon the terminology of networks and flows that had emerged a decade earlier. This new discourse was linked to the rapid growth of computer-based technologies at the center of what came to be known as the Information and Communication Revolution. At the time, Manuel Castells developed an influential framework that integrated the technological discourse centered on electronically processed information networks with globalization theory, configured around social interconnectivities and mobilities. Moreo-

> **Manuel Castells (1942–)** is Professor of Sociology at the Open University of Catalonia, Spain, and the Wallis Annenberg Chair of Communication Technology and Society at the University of Southern California, USA. His academic expertise includes media and communications, sociology, education, urban studies, and global studies. From 2020 to 2021, he served as Minister of Universities in the Spanish national government. In his pathbreaking three-volume study *The Information Age* (1996–98), Castells examines complex globalization processes across the major social domains of economics, politics, and culture. He argues that profound social transformations in the late twentieth century have facilitated the rise of a new social structure he calls the *global network society*. In his later work, he combines this analysis of network complexity with in-depth investigations of the new economy centered on digital information and communication technologies, the rise and fall of global social movements, and the expansion of *network power* by globally connected social elites.

ver, the Spanish communications scholar combined his complexity thinking skills with his efforts to establish a more empirically grounded account of globalization processes.

Castells's most basic idea is that of a *network*, which he defines as a set of *nodes* interconnected by *ties*. Particularly important nodes are called *centers* or *hubs*. Their functions depend on the programs that assign various goals and rules of performance, and on their interactions with other nodes in the network. Although networks are complex structures capable of organizing multidirectional and open-ended *flows* of information, people, things, and institutions, they work on a binary logic of *inclusion versus exclusion*. This means that, within the network, distance between interconnected nodes is zero, whereas for actors outside the network it is infinite since they have no access to the network unless the program allows it. In everyday social life, networks function very differently from centralized and hierarchically organized structures. They are complex webs of horizontal communicative interconnections fostering both cooperation and competition among internal users and, potentially, with external agents. Crucially, social coordination is achieved via the adoption of shared standards—ideas, norms, practices, points of reference, customs, rules, laws, and regulations—that enable network members to share information and achieve forms of reciprocity, exchange, and collective effort. Indeed, standards are central to the maintenance and growth of a network because they are common to all its members.[17]

Although networks have existed in various forms throughout human history, Castells emphasizes that their current manifestations are significantly more complex and expansive. Their unprecedented combination of flexibility and swift task-implementation sets them apart from other organizational types such as business-oriented markets and hierarchical bureaucracies.[18] Indeed, their inherent agility allows for a superior coordination and management of growing social complexity. Globalizing networks appear in contemporary social life in myriad forms and variations. For example, they serve as conduits for the capitalist world economy greased by transnational financial flows and round-the-clock stock markets. They can be globally connected webs of civil society and their proliferating nodes of information-sharing NGOs. They connect mobile digital devices that generate, transmit, and receive signals in gigantic

Complexity Theories / 121

social media systems. They appear in the production of new genetic engineering technologies or as expanding crime cartels and drug traffic routes cutting across national and regional geographies.

Presenting these new social networks as complex structures capable of global expansion and integration of an ever-larger number of nodes and ties, Castells argues that they have become animating forces of *all* dimensions of contemporary social life *everywhere* on the planet. This emerging *global network society* comprised of multiple smaller networks signals for Castells—as it does for Martin Albrow—the arrival of a radically new period in human history: the *Information Age*. Linked to the global expansion of capitalism based on new digital technologies, this new epoch has replaced the *Industrial Age* and its centrally organized, hierarchical chains of command and control geared toward the production and distribution of energy.[19]

Global networks form an intrinsic part of the dawning Information Age because they enhance cross-border interconnectivity and mobility. The global economy, in particular, both shapes and relies on networks, which enhance the flexibility and profitability of production of new forms of economic organization. Similar to Sassen's analysis, Castells approaches these emerging capitalist *network enterprises* as crucial nodes in multiscalar assemblages that apply to both large, internally decentralized corporations and medium to smaller firms connected to overarching networks and business alliances.[20]

Although Castells emphasizes the special significance of digital communication networks for global capitalism, he is careful to note that the impacts of the new communication technologies should not be reduced to deterministic explanations of globalization as technology plus markets. While the evolution of digital technology in the Information Age facilitates the formation of *informational capitalism*, it has also sparked a series of fundamental cultural and political transformations.[21] For example, global communication networks have significantly raised the level of reflexivity among ordinary citizens around the world who demand greater individual freedoms as well as the fulfillment of their material needs and desires. Overall, then, the rapid development of communication technology—together with the transformation of the social environment in which such communication occurs—also encourages new forms of meaning construction, and therefore the production of novel cultural forms.

To be sure, Castells's theory of the global network society raises as many new questions as it tries to answer. For example, how do sophisticated technologies of networked information and communication mediate the vast array of social, political, and economic practices? How, precisely, do global networks that operate primarily in one social domain interact with networks unfolding in other dimensions? And how do networks operate across different spatial scales? The key to answering these questions about the evolving global network society—and the diffusion of its logic of interconnectivity across all social domains—lies for Castells in gaining a better understanding of globalizing forms of social *complexity*. As he explains:

> Digital networking technologies, characteristic of the Information Age, powered social and organizational networks in ways that allowed their endless expansion and reconfiguration, overcoming the traditional limitations of networking forms of organization to *manage complexity* beyond a certain size of the network. Because networks do not stop at the border of the nation-state, the network society constitutes itself as a global system, ushering in the new form of globalization characteristic of our time.[22]

Complexity Theories / 123

In particular, Castells seeks to understand the increasing complexities of the global network society by analyzing *flows*. As we noted, these purposeful and repetitive sequences of exchange and interaction passing through nodes of the network involve all sorts of phenomena ranging from encrypted information to political refugees. Under conditions of increasing global complexity, flows can assume many different forms, characteristics, and qualities. For example, they can be constant or intermittent, isolated or reciprocal, one- or multidirectional, balanced or imbalanced, strong or weak.[23] Castells recognizes the difficulty of addressing all of these aspects and acknowledges the importance of limiting his empirical analysis to *specific* flows in the global network society. However, such focused inquiries cannot proceed without a prior consideration of larger space-time transformations in the human experience resulting from the globalizing patterns of interconnectedness and mobility.

Hence, the examination of new modes and dimensions of space and time mediated by information technologies assumes great significance in Castells's global network society framework. Once again, considerations of complexity are at the heart of his theorizing. Castells considers cross-border activity in the Information Age as a *space of flows*. He argues that microelectronics-based digital communication, advanced telecommunication networks, and computerized information systems have transformed conventional forms of social space by "introducing simultaneity, or any chosen time frame, in social practices, regardless of the location of the actors engaged in the communication process." Unlike the conventional *space of places*—bounded space linked to specific locations such as clearly delineated suburbs, villages, towns, and nation-states—space of flows refers to a new interrelationship of capital, knowledge, power, and communication that "involves the production, transmission, and processing of flows of information." Although the space of *digital* flows still relies on the production of place-based localities as nodes of expanding communication networks, the primary function of such places is limited to providing material support of simultaneous social practices communicated at a distance.[24] Influenced by Sassen, Castells observes that the global financial network, for example, is organized as flows connecting institutions located in global cities such as New York, London, and Shanghai.[25]

Moreover, Castells argues that intricate spatial flows are linked to corresponding temporal reconfigurations he calls *timeless time*.[26] This complex formation breaks with the logic of *sequence* as the traditional basis for ordering temporality, which represents the hallmark of modern time as the demarcated, linear, and empty time of the calendar and clock. In contrast to the rhythm of biological time characteristic of the Industrial Age, the timeless time of the Information Age is a mix of multiple temporalities that compress and reorganize events into past, present, and future instances in random sequences. As examples, Castells cites electronic hypertexts and the blurring of conventional life-cycle patterns in both work and private life.[27]

Driven by the accelerating ICT and AI revolution, today's shift toward timeless time becomes a mundane occurrence in digitally mediated activities such as the recording and retrieving of events for later action or the instantaneous electronic purchase in the globalized marketplace dominated by digital retailers like Amazon. The global reconfigurations of bounded space and sequenced time as the space of lows and timeless time enable the billions of transactions on Wall Street just as much as they impose a nonregressive discipline on the millions of bidders on eBay. They affect local real estate auctions as much as motion-sensitive traffic lights.

To sum up, the global network society reorganizes and manages social complexity through the space of flows and timeless time. Localized constraints of place and time no longer limit expanding and proliferating manifestations of human activity mediated by global communication networks. Still, Castells's complexity mode of theorizing not only recognizes the significance of cyberspace, but also acknowledges the materiality inherent in the space of flows. Crucially, he points to the rise of a flexible new economy organized in countless circuits of electronic exchanges that direct billions of financial transactions around the world. The formation of significant nodes and hubs in global cities not only facilitates the global division of labor, but also serves as crucial social meeting places for global elites. In short, the global network society is never switched off and the placement of its nodes in territorial space is less important than its existence as a space of flows where social activities take place. At the same time, Castells concedes that conventional modalities of space and time have been overlaid by the space of flows and timeless time without erasing them. Although instantaneity and proximity have become the new modes in the global age, they continue to cohabit our globalizing world with traditional forms of space and time.

In his later work, Castells consciously broadens his complexity thinking beyond his earlier focus on the dynamics of global capitalism to power dynamics in general. His analysis of the global network society allows him not only to explain how networks generate and manage multiple layers of social complexity, but also to identify intricate dynamics of inclusion and exclusion that shape a "geography of social, economic, and technological inequality." Thus, his construction of a *network theory of power* moves to the center of his research efforts.[28]

Castells distinguishes between four different forms of power that operate in the Information Age. *Networking power* is the power of the privileged actors included in the network over those who are excluded from it. *Network power* is exercised by the imposition of the rules of inclusion by insiders. *Networked power* refers to the power differential between certain social actors over others *within* the network. Finally, *network-making power* is both the power to program specific networks according to the interests of the privileged members and the power to switch to different networks following the strategic alliances between dominant actors of various networks.[29] In particular, Castells focuses on the exercise of hegemonic power by social elites who create and program political, military, and financial networks. While the network theory of power concentrates on the role of social elites, it also pays attention to the enactment of counter-power by dominated groups willing to disrupt prevailing networks and reprogram them around alternative interests and values.

This significant expansion of Castells's complexity thinking into the world of social movements and identity politics brings his theory closer to his transdisciplinary goal of examining different domains of the global network society to provide a more holistic understanding of "the trends that characterize the structure and dynamics of our societies in the world of the twenty-first century."[30] At the same time, however, such holistic attempts to lift the separate dimensions of globalization to a higher level of analysis cross over into the generalizing style of thinking. We return to this point in the concluding section of this chapter.

LIQUIFYING GLOBALIZATION

Building on the complexity approach of Castells's theory of the global network society, John Urry emerged in the 2000s as one of the most influential academic voices urging the infusion of globalization theory with insights drawn from complexity science. Crucially, he argues that new concepts and methods borrowed from physics and biology have the capacity to expand our understanding of the global as a complex system linked to a series of other interdependent systems.

While showing appreciation of Castells's innovative examination of intricately intersecting global networks as a new framework for studying globalization, Urry nonetheless criticizes his colleague for lacking a set of interrelated concepts that would broaden our understanding of *global complexity*. In particular, he deems Castells's key term *network* too undifferentiated to capture the multiplicity of the liquifying impacts of globalization on familiar social arrangements.[31] In other words, a discerning analysis of the global age cannot be reduced to a single core concept such as Castells's "network" or Hardt and Negri's "Empire." Instead, Urry chooses a different approach geared toward the overcoming of the "limitations of many globalization analyses that deal insufficiently with the *complex* character of emergent global relations."[32] Accordingly, he introduces at the center of his complexity thinking three new metaphors that stand for different *modes of networked relationships*.

First, Urry argues that emergent global systems contain interdependent and self-organizing *global hybrids*, which should be the primary subject matter of globalization theory in the twenty-first century. Combining both material and social relations in often unexpected ways, these assemblages are capable of

> **John Urry (1946–2016)** was Professor of Sociology at Lancaster University, UK. In addition to globalization theory, his areas of interest included environmental sociology, mobility and tourism studies, urban studies, future studies, and political economy. He is especially known for his pioneering efforts to bring notions of complexity and chaos from the natural sciences to the social sciences to illuminate intricate globalization processes. In his later work, Urry applied his framework of global complexity to the study of different forms of cross-boundary mobilities. In particular, he emphasized the transformative impact of globalization on the enhanced mobility of people, commodities, technologies, and ideas. Urry was also the founding editor of *Mobilities*, a leading journal in the transdisciplinary field of mobilities studies.

evolving toward both disorganization and order. Always teetering on the edge of chaos, global hybrids tend to move away from temporary points of equilibrium and stability. Thus, they exhibit the qualities of unpredictability, contingency, nonlinearity, irreversibility, and indeterminacy that have long been described and analyzed in complexity science.[33] Examples of global hybrids abound and include informational systems, "automobility," global media, the Internet, global climate change, transboundary health hazards, and international protests.

Next, Urry argues that these global hybrids form the crucial nodes in what he calls *globally integrated networks* (GINs). These complex configurations consist of networked connections between peoples, objects, and technologies stretching across multiple and distant spaces and times. The purpose of GINs is to manage global complexity by introducing temporary regularity and stability into the unpredictable unfolding of emergent globality. Urry argues that global enterprises like McDonald's, American Express, and Sony are organized through GINs. These corporations interweave technologies, skills, texts, and brands to ensure that the same service or product is delivered more or less the same way across the entire network. This makes desired outcomes more calculable, routinized, and standardized.

However, Urry also notes that GINs show weaknesses under conditions of advanced globalization. For example, the power of a global brand like Toyota based within a GIN can be reduced almost overnight as a consequence of relatively minor defects that result in mass recalls of the flawed vehicles. Other examples are local protests against global sweatshop practices or locally organized resistances to global corporations such as Starbucks, which produce unpredictable effects that are difficult to analyze within Castells's global network framework. Finally, Urry notes that large TNCs like Apple and Microsoft, which are organized through GINs, sometimes fail to react quickly to social challenges or rapidly changing consumer preferences. Such instances of inflexibility show that transnational corporations and other large networked institutions still exhibit insufficient flexibility and fluidity to implement more flexible modes of organizational coordination.[34] Urry's main point here is that, under conditions of intensifying globalization, a single network metaphor no longer suffices as an explanatory model of growing social complexity.

To remedy this shortcoming, Urry introduces his third, and perhaps most significant, key concept to the study of globalization: *global fluids* (GFs). While these highly evolved manifestations of complex global hybrids involve networks, Urry considers this term inadequate to characterize the uneven, emergent, and unpredictable shapes that fluids can assume. Structured by the intersecting domains of the global system, GFs of diverse viscosity travel along network ties from node to node and both organize and restructure the "messy power of complexity processes." Although GFs result from everyday people acting on the basis of local information, their actions impact distant places. Urry notes that the movements of GFs are much less stable and predictable than Castells suggests when he introduces the notion of the space of flows within the global network society. Rather, GFs "may escape, rather like white blood corpuscles, through the 'wall' into surrounding matter and effect unpredictable consequences upon the matter."[35]

Seizing upon the insight of quantum physics that matter exhibits qualities of both *particles and waves*, Urry proposes that GFs are constituted by particles/waves of increasing global complexity. They move "within and across diverse regions forming heterogeneous, uneven, unpredictable and often unplanned waves." For example, powerful fluids of traveling people or health hazards such as oil spills and global pandemics flow across borders at changing speeds and at different levels of viscosity with no necessary end state or ultimate purpose. Unlike Castells's network metaphor, Urry employs his key concept of GFs with the aim of explaining how global complexity is managed over time by creating its own context for action rather than being caused by specific contexts.[36] For Urry, then, the advantage of substituting his new global fluids metaphor for the more conventional notion of network flows lies in its superior representational powers. GFs provide researchers with a better conceptual grasp of the intersecting dynamics of globalization and their complex and ultimately unpredictable outcomes.

Troubled by the ambitious attempts of generalizing thinkers to produce a unitary theory of globalization, Urry suggests that globalization theory should be neither unified nor presented as a linear and orderly set of processes unfolding in different domains. His intellectual modesty is reflected in his acceptance of *limits to knowledge* that are inherent in the nature of growing global complexity itself. However, accepting limits does not mean abandoning the theoretical task of broadening one's knowledge of evolving GINs and GFs. Rather, Urry encourages fellow thinkers to proceed in a thoroughgoing postdisciplinary way that transcends the conventional divide between the natural and social sciences. In fact, such unorthodox inquiries into the complexity of contemporary global relations should become the default mode of globalization theory.[37]

CONCLUDING CRITICAL REFLECTIONS

Of all the modes of theorizing introduced in this book, the complexity style is arguably the most appropriate way of approaching such an astonishingly intricate and diverse set of processes as globalization. After all, a focus on complexity places multiple flows, networks, and fluids within a conceptual framework capable of accommodating a plethora of seemingly contradictory processes of integration and differentiation.

A second advantage of the complexity mode is its keen attention to the impact of digital technology on globalization and vice versa. As our world is seemingly becoming more dominated by digital systems of all sort—including AI and genetic engineering—a stronger orientation toward new forms of technology makes much sense. At the same time, however, complexity thinkers like Castells have to be careful not to become too technocentric in their approach. Indeed, his heavy reliance on the crucial role of ICT in a globalized world sometimes translates into a rather uncritical glorification of digitization and informationalism.

A third virtue of complexity thinking is its flexible applicability to the three levels of analysis—micro, mid-range, and macro—as well as its resonance with all of the major domains of globalization.

Fourth, the complexity mode easily intersects with other styles of theorizing globalization. As we have seen, John Urry combines it with critical thinking. Sassen and Harvey connect it to their respective domain analyses of the global economy. Castells appears to be quite tempted to interweave it with a generalizing inquiry into the multidimensional dynamics of the global network society. Of these three complexity theorists, Castells is thus most in danger of producing the kind of grand theory of globalization that runs counter to more nuanced reflections that put complexity at the center of the study of worldwide interconnectivities and mobilities.

A fifth virtue of complexity thinking lies in its ability to bridge the conventional gulf that separates the natural and social sciences. A common research focus on complexity allows social theorists to familiarize themselves with concepts and models linked to uncertainty, multiplicity, indeterminacy, randomness, unpredictability, and relativity that have long been staples in such disciplines as physics, biology, and mathematics. Importing these scientific insights to the social arena also makes it easier for scholars to break down the limiting framework of methodological nationalism and instead present transnational social relations as complex systems of interconnections that operate simultaneously on multiple spatial scales and across different temporalities. Moreover, the growing convergence of the

Figure 13. The new vocabulary of global complexity

sciences and humanities facilitated by complexity thinking invites innovative transdisciplinary projects intent on solving concrete global problems rather than self-serving defenses of disciplinary silo-thinking.

Finally, the ongoing unsettling of the nature/nurture divide has introduced an entirely new vocabulary into globalization theory. As the complexity perspectives discussed in this chapter demonstrate, this innovative conceptual toolbox has already been put to good use and yielded valuable insights. Crucially, it has helped to provide better explanations for why globalization should no longer be constructed as a linear and orderly set of processes unfolding primarily in the economic domain.

On the flipside, however, there are also a number of problems with the new vocabulary of global complexity. First, it consists of a large number of often overlapping concepts that engage complexity in rather abstract ways. Similar to the generalizing style of thinking, the high level of abstraction associated with complexity theory makes it hard for nonspecialists to understand how, exactly, metaphors like globally integrated networks and global fluids are related and work in practice. Indeed, this rather dense and abstract set of concepts is often employed in the service of arguments that provide little by way of real-world illustration and specification. As a result, then, the new idiom of global complexity easily obscures the connections between theory and practice, which are of vital importance for the engagement of global problems.

Second, the discursive emphasis on networks, fluidity, and multiple spatial scales raises the old *structure versus agency problem* in the social sciences. If global networks are self-organizing structures, how much human agency—if any—is there in our globalizing world? The model of detached network operations described by complexity metaphors of contingency and chaos also tends to overemphasize discontinuity and randomness at the expense of continuities and causal determinations.

Third, the employment of an abstract set of complexity metaphors sometimes favors arguments by assertion rather than a discourse on the basis of empirical evidence. While it seems fair to claim that complexity thinking challenges traditional causal and determinate reasoning, it is nonetheless incumbent upon the complexity researcher to offer alternative *explanations* that expand our knowledge of the global, not to speak of constructive ways of solving global problems. As the social theorist Gregor McLennan points out, skeptics of complexity thinking should at least be entitled to ask how scholars who favor uncertainty, unpredictability, and spontaneity *know* that global fluids display distinct viscosities, speeds, directions, and temporalities.[38]

Fourth, the investigation of globalization through the new language of global complexity demands the theorist's acceptance of the impossibility of closure in the analysis of globalization. The resulting imperative of intellectual modesty that comes with the recognition of limits to knowledge tends to be obeyed by only the rarest of globalization theorists such as John Urry.

One final weakness of complexity theory has also shadowed our previous discussion of the general and domain mode of theorizing: Eurocentrism. All of the globalization thinkers discussed in this chapter employ the complexity mode within the framework of Western modernity. This persistent problem is all the more vexing in the broader context of complexity theory as it emerged from the natural sciences. After all, prominent quantum physicists like Fritjof Capra and David Bohm have been careful to link their discussions of complexity to the philosophical and cosmological frameworks that frame Eastern religions such as Buddhism, Taoism, and Hinduism. As postcolonial critics covered in the next chapter point out, complexity theorists of globalization—just like generalists and domain thinkers—have much to catch up on in this respect.

NOTES

1. Stephen Hawking, *A Brief History of Time* (London: Bantam, 1988), 33.

2. David Bohm cited in John Urry, *Global Complexity* (Cambridge, UK: Polity Press, 2003), 20.

3. Werner Heisenberg cited in Fritjof Capra, *The Web of Life: A New Scientific Understanding of Living Systems* (New York: Anchor, 1996), 30.

4. John R. Turner and Rose M. Baker, "Complexity Theory: An Overview with Potential Applications for the Social Sciences," *Systems* 7, no. 4 (2019): 4.

5. Ilya Prigogine, *The End of Certainty* (New York: The Free Press, 1997), 30.

6. See www.santafe.edu/about/overview.

136 / *Complexity Theories*

7. Marshall McLuhan, *Understanding Media: The Extension of Man*, reprint ed. (Cambridge, MA: MIT Press, 1994), 3.

8. See Warwick E. Murray, *Geographies of Globalization* (London: Routledge, 2006).

9. Henri Lefebvre, *The Production of Space* (Oxford, UK: Blackwell, 1991), 335, 422, my emphasis.

10. Saskia Sassen, "Globalization or Denationalization?," *Review of International Political Economy* 10, no. 1 (February 2003): 1–4.

11. Saskia Sassen, *A Sociology of Globalization* (New York: W. W. Norton, 2007), 18.

12. Saskia Sassen, *The Global City: New York, London, Tokyo*, 2nd ed. (Princeton, NJ: Princeton University Press, 2001), xviii–xix.

13. David Harvey, "Globalization and the 'Spatial Fix'," *Geographische Review* 2 (2001): 29.

14. Sassen, *Global City*, 3–4.

15. Saskia Sassen, *Territory, Authority, Rights: From Medieval to Global Assemblages* (Princeton, NJ: Princeton University Press, 2008), 345; Sassen, *Sociology of Globalization*, 102.

16. Saskia Sassen, *Expulsions: Brutality and Complexity in the Global Economy* (Cambridge, MA: Harvard University Press, 2014).

17. Manuel Castells, *The Rise of the Network Society*, vol. 1 of *The Information Age: Economy, Society, and Culture*, 2nd. ed. (Chichester, UK: Wiley-Blackwell, 2010); Castells, *Communication Power* (Oxford, UK: Oxford University Press, 2009), 19–21. See also David Grewal Singh, *Network Power: The Social Dynamics of Globalization* (New Haven, CT: Yale University Press, 2008).

18. Robert J. Holton, *Global Networks* (Houndmills, UK: Palgrave Macmillan, 2008), 4.

19. Manuel Castells, "Materials for an Exploratory Theory of the Network Society," *British Journal of Sociology* 51, no. 1 (January/March 2000): 5–24.

20. Castells, 10–11.

21. Castells, *Rise of the Network Society*, xviii, 6.

22. Castells, 6, my emphasis.

23. Darin Barney, *The Network Society* (Cambridge, UK: Polity Press, 2004), 26.

24. Castells, *Rise of the Network Society*, xxxii.

25. Holton, *Global Networks*, 19.

26. Castells, *Rise of the Network Society*, xl–xli.

27. Castells, "Materials for an Exploratory Theory," 13–14.

28. See Castells, *Communication Power*; Castells, "A Network Theory of Power," *International Journal of Communication* 5 (2011), 773–87; and Manuel Castells, *Networks of Outrage and Hope: Social Movements in the Internet Age* (Cambridge, UK: Polity Press, 2012).

29. Manuel Castells, *Communication Power*, 2nd ed. (Oxford, UK; Oxford University Press, 2009).

30. Castells, *Rise of the Network Society*, xix.

31. Here, Urry draws on the notion of *liquid modernity* coined by the sociologist Zygmunt Bauman in *Liquid Modernity* (Cambridge, UK: Polity Press, 2000).

32. John Urry, *Global Complexity* (Cambridge, UK: Polity Press, 2003), 39.

33. Urry, 14.

34. Urry, 56–59.

35. Urry, 60.

36. Urry, 60–61.

37. Urry, 124.

38. Gregor McLennan, "Sociology's Complexity," *Sociology* 37, no. 3 (2003): 556.

CHAPTER FOUR

Critical Theories

This chapter introduces theories of globalization designed and executed in a critical mode of inquiry. After an initial explanation of *critical theory* and its primary features, the chapter provides a brief review of two influential critiques of globalization theory made by scholars outside the field.

We start with an examination of Justin Rosenberg's argument that globalization theorists have not offered precise enough definitions of globalization theory's core concepts to allow for the formulation of *clear scientific propositions*. According to Rosenberg, a major consequence of such sloppy analytical draftsmanship is that many thinkers use the term indiscriminately to ascribe almost anything to "globalization." Finally, he notes that this definitional murkiness also applies to circular understandings of globalization as both as a cause and an outcome.

Next, we consider Paul Hirst and Grahame Thompson's similar critique of globalization as an imprecise and inflated term. Examining the relevance of this analytical problem to the economic domain, the two scholars argue that the world economy is far from being genuinely global. They cite empirical data to show that trade, investment, and financial flows are highly concentrated in Europe, North America, and East Asia. Thus, economic globalization is a misnomer for what, at best, should be seen as a *regional phenomenon* manifested in trading blocs and production chains that operate at various subglobal levels.

We then turn from criticisms of globalization theory made by scholars outside the field to examine two critical styles of theorizing utilized by insiders. The first perspective is exemplified by James Mittelman's contestation of *social injustices* and *inequalities* created by neoliberal capitalist globalization. His innovative framework of a *critical globalization theory* emerges as the result of several intellectual maneuvers such as scrutinizing the narratives and discourses used to frame globalizing processes; probing the institutional practices that enable the creation of knowledge and ideologies; closely attending to concrete cultural contexts; listening to marginalized voices; engaging in social practices of resisting arbitrary power; and promoting global citizenship. Mittelman's critical style of theorizing connects the production of knowledge to the emancipatory struggles of the global justice movement.

The second type of internal criticisms draws on the insights of *postcolonial and indigenous theory* to address the pervasive Eurocentric biases in globalization theory referred to in previous chapters. Postcolonial globalization critics like Walter Mignolo and Boaventura de Sousa Santos call for the greater inclusion of Global South perspectives articulated by marginalized thinkers who reject Western modernity and its violent legacy of imperialism and colonialism. Mignolo's critical intervention, in particular, suggests that most globalization scholars employing various styles of theorizing have not paid enough attention to the ethical imperative of deconstructing the dominant Western ways of seeing and knowing.

As in previous chapters, we end our discussion with an evaluation of some major strengths and weaknesses of the critical mode of theorizing globalization.

THE CRITICAL MODE OF THEORIZING

One can find different understandings of *critical thinking* in the academic world today. Originally, the term *critical* derives from the ancient Greek verb *krinein*, which translates in various ways as "to judge," "to discern," "to separate," and "to decide." The compound *critical thinking*, then, refers to a mode of thought intent on assessing the qualities of a thing or person in a discerning way. Modern social thinkers have pointed to a strong philosophical affinity between *critical* and *thinking*, but the conceptual connection between these terms goes back for millennia. Both Western and Eastern cultural traditions have celebrated the virtues of critical thinking as epitomized in such heroic tomes as Plato's *Republic* and the Hindu *Bhagavad Gita*. Indeed, these philosophical traditions do not understand critical thinking solely in *analytic* terms as *value-free* operations of the logical mind, but recognize that it also entails ethical norms that can translate into political commitments.

Yet, these vital moral dimensions and implications of discerning thought were often given secondary status in the new *critical thinking framework* created by leading Anglo-American educators during the second half of the twentieth century. Turning an old philosophical ideal into a popular educational catchphrase, these pedagogues equated the task of enabling students to think critically with a teachable scientific method of detached and self-directed reasoning. Such critical thinking was said to express itself in balanced and value-neutral cognitive operations like "seeing both sides of an issue, being open to new evidence that disconfirms your ideas, reasoning dispassionately, demanding that claims be backed by evidence, deducing and inferring conclusions from available facts, solving problems, and so forth."[1]

Undoubtedly, the analytical capabilities of objectivity, balance, and problem-solving should be part of any form of critical thinking. At the same time, however, the well-meaning efforts of pedagogues to enhance the educational effectiveness of their vocation should not remain unconcerned with political and ethical reflexivity, lest they reduce the activity of critical thinking to a mere analytical skill. Indeed, the presentation of critical activity as a neutral form of cognitive dexterity betrays a rather impoverished social and ethical imagination. Confined to such a value-free analytic framework, critical thinking connects to the everyday lifeworld only in rather instrumental ways. Hence, it resonates with the exhortations of many business leaders in capitalist societies who demand of schools that they improve students' critical thinking skills in the hope of taking material advantage of a well-educated workforce. Other than making more profitable work-related judgments, however, the notion of "well-educated" in this neoliberal context has no explicit ethical content. Rather, it refers to economic efficiency, productivity, flexibility, and other instrumental skills highly valued by global capitalism.

Conversely, ethical and political understandings of critical thinking emphasize the crucial link between thinking and its engaged social practices. Thought processes should not be isolated from the normative dimensions of the human experience. It is not enough to engage things merely in terms of how they are but also how they ought to be. And being mindful of this socially engaged dimension of critical thinking also means being aware of the connection between introspection and action. Ultimately, it makes sense to conceptualize the interrelation between analytical and ethical dimensions as *Stage 1* and *Stage 2 of critical thinking.*

As the French sociologist Pierre Bourdieu emphasizes, "Today's researchers must innovate an improbable but indispensable combination: *scholarship with commitment*, that is, a collective politics of intervention in the political field that follows, as much as possible, the rules that govern the scientific field." However, it is important to note that Bourdieu's willingness to follow, as much as possible, the scientific logic of objective science shows his respect for the Stage 1 analytical dimension of critical thinking. At the same time, he is equally clear that academics ought not remain in such socially neutral territory, but should be prepared to integrate Stage 2 in critical thinking: the acceptance of their ethical obligation as *public intellectuals* to contest all forms of domination and exploitation by special power interests. Ultimately, Bourdieu likens scholarly intervention in the social world on behalf of the powerless to a symbolic act of giving moral force to critical ideas and analyses.[2]

Focusing on the crucial link between theory and practice has served as common ground for various socially engaged currents of critical thinking that are often subsumed under the general category of critical theory. Originally used in the singular and upper case, *Critical Theory* is associated with mid-twentieth-century articulations of neo-Marxism as developed by three generations of thinkers of the Frankfurt School of Social Research in Germany. Rejecting the Marxist orthodoxy of economic determinism as well as the authoritarianism of Soviet commu-

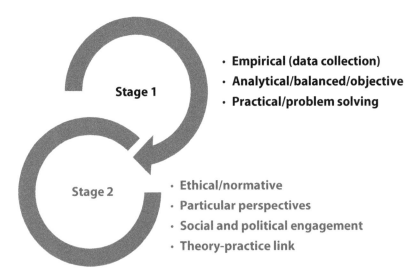

Figure 14. Two stages of critical thinking

nism, Critical Theorists promoted a democratic understanding of the emancipatory role of critical thinking in the class struggle for social justice and against oppressive forms of alienation, commodification, and conformity generated in advanced capitalist societies.[3]

Since the 1970s, the Critical Theory tradition of the Frankfurt School has been subsumed under a significantly expanded umbrella of *critical theories*—used in the plural and in lower case. These proliferating variations now stretch across an extremely wide intellectual terrain. They not only cover conventional class-based perspectives, but also include more current identity-centered critical perspectives ranging from feminist theory and queer theory to psychoanalytic theory; from poststructuralism and postcolonialism to indigenous thought; and from literary criticism and critical legal studies to critical race theory.

144 / *Critical Theories*

Such growing methodological diversity and philosophical eclecticism notwithstanding, many of today's critical theorists take as their common point of departure the specific social contexts to analyze the dynamics of unaccountable power, domination, exploitation, and injustice.

Globalization theory has been significantly framed by Critical Theory and the proliferation of critical theories. It assigns a special obligation to globalization thinkers not only to cast a more discerning spotlight on the dynamics of social injustice that are affecting our daily lives, but also to take seriously important criticisms leveled by external observers against their field. At their best, such critiques by outsiders contribute to the correction of flawed models, the illumination of blind spots and omissions, and the detection of theoretical pitfalls and dead ends.

Hence, before we explore two influential critical strands of theorizing globalization, let us briefly consider two such external criticisms directed against the core of globalization theory itself. One of the most radical of these challenges appears in the work of Justin Rosenberg. It amounts to an outright dismissal of the utility of globalization as an explanatory scheme in its own right. An example of the second, more moderate, criticism can be found in Paul Hirst and Grahame Thompson's reproach of globalization theory as an overblown framework that exaggerates both the intensity and extensity of existing economic networks. In their view, much of globalization theory amounts to little more than *globaloney*.[4]

DISMISSING GLOBALIZATION

Rosenberg's radical challenge to globalization theory starts with his assertion that globalization fails the three most basic

Critical Theories / 145

intellectual requirements of an *explanatory* concept in the social sciences.[5] First, any such keyword should be clearly and coherently defined. Reviewing influential definitions offered by prominent globalization theorists—including those of Giddens and Scholte—Rosenberg concludes that their suggested meanings remain murky and elusive. To buttress this negative assessment, he observes that even globalization thinkers themselves seem to agree on the contentious nature of basic definitional matters in their field. Here, Rosenberg echoes similar criticisms made by previous globalization skeptics, who consider globalization a prime example of a "vacuous" and "amorphous" idea resting on "slim foundations" and used in academic discourses to refer to "anything from the Internet to a hamburger."[6]

Rosenberg connects these definitional problems to the second alleged failure of globalization theory, which is reflected in its inability to derive intelligible hypotheses from its amorphous key concept. He cites as an example of this flaw one of the most basic hypotheses of globalization theory: globalization undermines state sovereignty. As we noted in previous chapters, this claim had been advanced by deterritorialization thinkers like Giddens, Scholte, and Sassen, and many others. Conversely, Rosenberg highlights a contradiction in their related call for a shift from methodological nationalism to methodological globalism: the concession that globalization's intermingling and dissolution of nested geographical scales does not negate the enduring significance of the nation-state as the most relevant site of political power.

If the globalization hypothesis of deterritorialization is to mean anything, Rosenberg asks, must it not be manifested in the waning of bounded entities such as the sovereign nation-state? Since such a fundamental transformation cannot be confirmed

> **Justin Rosenberg (1960–)** is Professor Emeritus of International Relations at the University of Sussex, UK. From 2011 to 2014, he served at this institution as head of the Department of International Relations. His academic areas of expertise span international theory, world history, development theory, social theories of modernity, and Marxism and international relations. Rosenberg uses a Marxist historical-materialist approach to critique globalization theory as well as liberal and realist strands of IR theory. He faults globalization theory for its alleged inability to offer causal explanations of contemporary social change. Ultimately, Rosenberg insists that globalization theory cannot be sustained as a new conceptual framework in the social sciences because it has not significantly advanced social knowledge beyond the pioneering insights articulated by classical social theorists like Karl Marx and Max Weber.

empirically, Rosenberg concludes that the best these globalization theorists can do is to point to limited forms of *regional* integration like the European Union. However, these voluntary associations have nothing specifically *global* about them, which means that the hypothesis of globalization as a driver of deterritorialization finds itself both analytically and empirically on shaky grounds.[7]

According to Rosenberg, the third failure of globalization theory is connected to the previous two weaknesses: the inability to apply the ill-defined core concept and its flawed hypotheses to concrete historical explanations. In his view, the third deficiency is especially visible in the frequent presentation of globalization as both the *outcome*—the social condition of worldwide interdependence—and a social *process* of expanding spatial relations leading to this outcome. This sloppy practice of associating globalization with such different things as a condition, a process, a force, or an age feeds what Rosenberg calls the biggest *folly of globalization theory*. It appears in the form of a circular reasoning process—globalization causes globalization—which has no explanatory value. For this reason, Rosenberg suggests that globalization should be restricted to its use as a *descriptive* category that merely *invokes* and *depicts* international phenomena. As an explanatory concept necessary for theory building, however, the term is "simply a non-starter, an empty piece of nothing."[8]

In the years of a globalization backlash following the terrorist attacks of September 11, 2001, Rosenberg published a lengthy "post mortem to globalization theory." Its central thesis states that the phenomenon has ceased to matter in the new century. The article even goes so far as to allege the intellectual bankruptcy of the entire theoretical edifice of globalization, adding that the much-touted worldwide compression of space and time probably never existed in the first place. And even if it did, Rosenberg concludes, there seems little doubt that "the 'age of globalization' is over … Globalization will become just another word for interdependence."[9]

This chapter is not the proper place to present some of the lengthy rejoinders to Rosenberg's alleged three failures of globalization theory.[10] However, since his claim of deficient definitions of globalization lies at the core of his criticism, it seems useful to offer just one brief counterargument on this point. Rosenberg is surely right to call out imprecise definitions that tend to refer to different global phenomena. In particular, the sloppy conflation of globalization as both a process and a condition has at times led to circular arguments that have no explanatory power and erase meaningful analytical distinctions between causes and effects.

But the problem of deficient definitions plagued globalization theory mostly in its infancy in the 1990s. When Rosenberg authored his series of external criticisms in the 2000s, there was no dearth of writings that include more precise definitions.[11] Most importantly, these definitions make clear distinctions between *globalization* as a concept referring to a social *process* and *globality* as a term signifying a social condition. As we noted in the introduction, this distinction is crucial, because it eliminates circular definitions by specifying that globalization refers to a set of social processes propelling us towards the condition of globality. Allowing for analytical distinctions between causes and effects, the distinction between these two terms seems to fit Rosenberg's rather narrow framework for explanatory concepts in the social sciences capable of generating clear hypotheses.

Let us now consider the second, more moderate, external criticism of globalization theory. This perspective is perhaps best reflected in the writings of the late Paul Hirst and his coauthor, Grahame Thompson. Like Rosenberg, the British political economists start their challenge by pointing to allegedly inflated definitions of globalization, which have drawn more and more aspects of the modern condition under their conceptual umbrella. In their ensuing domain analysis of economic globalization, these critics claim that the world economy is not a truly global phenomenon, but one centered on Europe, East Asia, and North America. They emphasize that the majority of economic activity around the world still remains primarily national in origin and scope, thus dismissing the same deterritorialization hypothesis that Rosenberg challenged in his analysis. Presenting ample empirical data on trade, foreign direct investment, and

Critical Theories / 149

financial flows, Hirst and Thompson warn against drawing global conclusions from increased levels of economic interaction in advanced industrial countries. Without a truly global economic system, they insist, there can be no such thing as globalization: "As we proceeded [with our economic research] our skepticism deepened until we became convinced that globalization, as conceived by the more extreme globalizers, is largely a myth."[12]

Buried under an avalanche of empirical data, one can also detect an incipient *normative* message in the Hirst–Thompson thesis: exaggerated accounts of economic globalization as overwhelming the nation-state are prone to produce disempowering political effects. For example, Hirst and Thompson point to neoliberal politicians who have used the claim of economic globalization to propose national economic deregulation and the reduction of welfare programs. And they go on to note that the implementation of such policies stands to benefit primarily corporate interests at the expense of poor people.

At the same time, however, one can find a number of problems with the moderate Hirst–Thompson critique of globalization theory. For starters, it sets overly high standards for the economy in order to be counted as fully globalized. Second, their efforts to construct an abstract model of a perfectly globalized economy unnecessarily polarizes the topic by pressuring the reader to either completely embrace or entirely reject the concept of globalization. But perhaps the most serious shortcoming of the Hirst–Thompson critique lies in their single-domain approach that makes globalization primarily an economic phenomenon. As a result, their narrative either glosses over other major dimensions of globalization—culture, politics, and ideology—or treats them in a neo-Marxist fashion as mere reflections of an underlying economic logic. While paying lip service to the multidimensional character of globalization, their own analysis ignores the logical implications of this recognition. After all, if globalization is truly a complex, multileveled phenomenon, then economic relations constitute only one among many globalizing dynamics. It would therefore be entirely possible to argue for the significance of globalization even if Hirst and Thompson managed to demonstrate empirically that increased transnational economic activity appears to be limited to advanced industrial countries.

Let us now turn from our brief presentation of *external* criticisms to a consideration of two *internal* modes of critical thinking employed by globalization theorists themselves. While approaching their subject from distinct thematic perspectives—the unmasking of global injustice in general and the integration of postcolonial and indigenous voices—these thinkers converge in their exposure and condemnation of asymmetrical power relations stretching across the globe. Their aim is to render global injustices and the marginalization of Global South perspectives unacceptable and thereby encourage social thinkers around the world to contribute to social change in the direction of emancipation from domination.[13] However, pursuing such a difficult goal does not mean the abandonment of empirical methodologies or qualitative methods such as *thick description* in favor of partisan polemics.[14] Rather, the objective of these theorists is to combine Stage 1 and Stage 2 modes of critical thinking to unmask exploitative global processes.

THEORIZING GLOBAL JUSTICE

As we discussed previously, dominant neoliberal elites have promoted the idea of globalization since the 1980s as a new paradigm capable of producing wealth and well-being for all. While corporate globalization did lift the incomes and living standards of millions in some emerging markets in Asia, it also delivered ecological degradation, new forms of militarism and digitalized surveillance, economic inequality, hyperconsumerism, and new forms of cultural commodification. These negative outcomes triggered large-scale public protests around the world and impacted the evolution of critical globalization thinking. Crucially, the mounting disaffection with neoliberal globalization created fertile conditions for the emergence of a powerful *global justice movement.* Its members advocated people-led forms of *globalization-from-below,* which most market globalists falsely characterized as "antiglobalization."

In particular, the Mexican *Zapatista Army of National Liberation*—originally formed by indigenous peoples in the southern state of Chiapas to protest the negative effects of the 1994 North American Free Trade Agreement—proved to be successful in transmitting their critical message to other social justice networks around the world. The resulting global *Zapatista Solidarity Network* exerted a profound influence on the 2001 founding and subsequent expansion of the *World Social Forum* (WSF) as an alternative to the neoliberal World Economic Forum in Davos, Switzerland. Designed as an open meeting place, the WSF encourages and facilitates a free exchange of ideas among scholars and activists dedicated to challenging *globalization-from-above.* Hundreds of WSF member organizations around the world construct and disseminate visions of an alternative form of globalization based on their core principles of equality, global social justice, diversity, democracy, nonviolence, solidarity, ecological sustainability, and planetary citizenship.[15]

This growing global justice movement inspired some globalization thinkers to assemble a new conceptual paradigm increasingly referred to as *critical globalization studies* or *critical theories of globalization*. The American sociologists Richard Appelbaum and William Robinson, for example, intertwined their domain mode of theorizing focused on the global capitalist economy with a constructive criticism that envisioned a new global order based on "a preferential option for the subordinate majority of emergent global society."[16] Emphasizing that critical globalization theory should be broad enough to house a variety of methodological approaches and knowledge systems, they argued that intellectual diversity should nonetheless serve the common goal of unmasking the exploitative practices of corporate capitalism.

For Appelbaum and Robinson, then, the goal of critical globalization thinking is the production of "self-knowledge of global society through active theorizing and political work."[17] Ideas should be explicitly linked to emancipatory social practices, especially to the building of bridges between socially engaged theory and the global justice movement. Ultimately, the value of critical globalization theory should be determined by its ability to inspire progressive social change. Appelbaum and Robinson sum up their critical style of inquiry in the following way: "We believe that as scholars it is incumbent upon us to explore the relevance of academic research to the burning political issues and social struggles of our epoch, and to the many conflicts, hardships, and hopes bound up with globalization. More directly stated, we are not indifferent observers studying globalization as a sort of detached academic exercise."[18]

Another version of critical globalization thinking focuses specifically on the role of subjective forms of consciousness in resisting the exercise of arbitrary power and ideological domination. Analyzing the various ways in which neoliberal globalization has been powering knowledge systems, James Mittelman is a leading

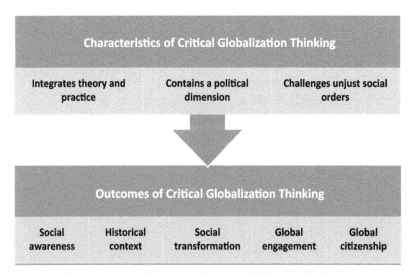

Figure 15. Characteristics and outcomes of critical globalization thinking

critic of neoliberal globalization who also investigates knowledge frameworks produced by various globalization scholars from around the world. His careful analysis of these models over many years provides the foundation for his conceptual framework of *critical globalization theory*. It consists of five interacting elements.[19]

The first component is *reflexivity*. Mittelman relates the meaning of the term specifically to an awareness of the relationship between knowledge production and specific material and political conditions. Hence, the formulation of critical globalization theory requires the development and refinement of a searching consciousness capable of probing the causes and manifestations of global transformations. Moreover, Mittelman insists that to be reflexive means to examine the specific historical context and power interests embedded in various globalization narratives.

> **James H. Mittelman (1944–)** is Distinguished Research Professor at American University, USA, and Honorary Fellow at the Helsinki Collegium for Advanced Studies, Finland. He served as a member of the Institute for Advanced Study in Princeton, USA, and held the Pok Rafeah Chair at the National University of Malaysia. As a trained IR theorist and African area specialist, he has also worked with the United Nations and various civil society organizations on development issues in the Global South. He is one of the earliest scholars to craft a critical style of theorizing globalization. One of Mittelman's most important theoretical contributions is his sophisticated recasting of globalization as a form of intellectual power manifested in neoliberal knowledge systems, which are primarily propagated and reproduced by Western social elites.

The critical scrutiny of historical globalization dynamics also relates to Mittelman's second component: *historicism*. Signifying awareness of the shifting conditions of history, this concept incorporates the time dimension in theorizing about globalization. It also corrects ahistorical approaches reflected in neoliberal claims about the alleged inevitability and irreversibility of global market integration. Mittelman emphasizes that critical globalization thinking must always proceed from definite historical locations, which allow for more discerning assessments of changing globalization processes and their inherent power relations.

Mittelman characterizes *transdisciplinarity*, the third element of critical globalization thinking, as the ability to forge *crossovers* between the social sciences and complementary branches of knowledge in the natural sciences and humanities. Productive of a critical understanding of globalization, crossovers are designed to encourage scholars to break through disciplinary barriers in their holistic pursuit of global problems such as pandemics, migration, and climate change.

Mittelman also links crossover thinking to educational activities directed at the cultivation of *global citizenship*. This term has been associated with educational initiatives seeking to inspire young people around the world to grow into morally responsible, intellectually competent, and culturally perceptive global citizens.[20] According to Mittelman, the promotion of global citizenship in the educational arena involves a number of elements: the cultivation of thinking beyond one's imagined physical boundaries toward a global consciousness of planetary interdependence, a sense of one's global responsibility and shared moral obligations across humankind, and the strengthening of democratic ideals of democratic empowerment and participation.[21] Noted globalization theorist Mark Juergensmeyer adds another piece by linking global citizenship to specific educational efforts to create *global literacy*—the ability of students to conduct critical examinations of specific aspects of diverse cultures and economic practices as well as other influential global trends and patterns.[22]

Strategic transformations, the fourth component of Mittelman's critical globalization theory, signals the researcher's willingness to present constructive challenges to the hegemonic power interests of the incipient global society. This means that the socially engaged thinkers behind these strategic maneuvers are key to developing emancipatory roadmaps that lead to more democratic forms of globalization. Drawing on the terminology

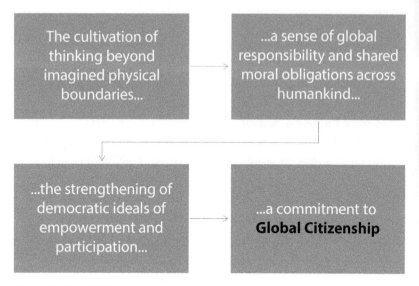

Figure 16. Global citizenship as a process

of the Italian cultural Marxist Antonio Gramsci, Mittelman characterizes critical globalization thinkers as "organic intellectuals" capable of speaking to a wider public and contributing to the generation of a "new common sense" about the negative consequences of neoliberal globalization. By linking their analyses to the production of a socially empowering pedagogy, organic intellectuals feed the "creative mills" of critical globalization theory committed to the production of alternative knowledge and a more egalitarian global future. As Mittelman emphasizes, "The goal is to inculcate a new moral order in lieu of the dominant ethos—currently an ethos of efficiency, competition, individualism, and consumption inscribed in neoliberalism."[23]

Mittelman refers to the final component of his critical globalization theory model as *decentering*. This critical thinking style involves the active inclusion of various forms of knowledge of globalization generated in the margins of the Global South. In his view, importing and applying such decentered postcolonial perspectives has the innovative potential to infuse existing criticisms of neoliberal globalization with new understandings derived from the populations in the Global South who suffer the most from the exploitative economic practices and oppressive knowledge systems of the West. Thus, the component of decentering relates Mittelman's overarching demand for greater global social justice to the necessary import of postcolonial and indigenous *epistemologies*—ways of knowing—into mainstream globalization theory. And it is to these pressing demands articulated by *postcolonial* and *indigenous* thinkers located mostly within the field of globalization theory that we must now turn.

INTEGRATING POSTCOLONIAL AND INDIGENOUS THEORIES

Postcolonial theory consists of a related set of perspectives and principles that involve a conceptual reorientation toward knowledges developed outside the West—in Asia, Africa, Oceania, and Latin America. By seeking to insert alternative knowledges into the dominant power structures of the Global North, postcolonial theorists attempt to change the way people think—and the way they behave—to produce more just and equitable global social relations. Emphasizing the connection between theory and practice, postcolonial intellectuals consider themselves critical thinkers who challenge the alleged superiority of Western cultures, racism and other forms of ethnic bias, economic inequality separating the Global North from the South, and the persistence of *orientalism*—a discriminatory, Europe-derived mindset so brilliantly dissected by late postcolonial theorist

Edward Said.[24] To sum up, then, postcolonialism is a socially engaged form of critical thinking "about a changing world, a world that has been changed by struggle and which its practitioners intend to change further."[25]

Similarly, *indigenous theories* and epistemologies present a challenge to the Enlightenment "truths" produced by a Eurocentric logic of objectivity and individualism. By contrast, indigenous ways of knowing prioritize communal lifestyles based on relational concepts of power. They contain strong ethical elements linked to the fundamental interdependence of specific places, ecologies, and life-systems. Overcoming the fundamental Western division between nature and society, indigenous thinkers and First Nation activists argue that decolonialization has not yet ended. Rather, it constitutes an ongoing process aimed at the return of land, power, and wealth into the hands of indigenous peoples. Genuine reconciliation is only possible by changing the colonizers' mentality of superiority reflected in lingering racist and violent attitudes. Ultimately, indigenous thinkers demand that their customary ways of knowing and being must be accorded the same value as Western epistemologies.[26]

If theorizing globalization from a Northern standpoint is not made explicit, it becomes complicit in larger forms of injustice that operate both on epistemological and ethical levels. Epistemologies are not lifeless abstractions, but mental models that have the power to create, shape, and destroy social environments. Unequal social and cultural exchanges rooted in racist ideas can culminate in what postcolonial scholar-activist Boaventura de Sousa Santos calls *epistemicide*: the annihilation of the entire knowledge system of the subordinate culture and the social groups that possessed it. In extreme cases such as the violent colonial practices of European powers, epistemicides of complex indigenous knowledges became one of the preconditions of genocides in the twentieth century. De Sousa Santos concludes that if the critical impulse is to survive, it is imperative for thinkers around the world to distance themselves from the old Eurocentric framework of Critical Theory that has provided only weak answers for the strong questions confronting humanity in the global age.[27] After all, even after the successful political decolonization processes of the twentieth century, the priority of Western knowledge systems has continued to be safeguarded by Euro-American universities.

De Sousa Santos and other postcolonial and indigenous theorists have inspired a wave of critical examinations of the connections between globalization and postcolonialism.[28] Most of these thinkers object to what they see as globalization theory's narrow geographic, ethnic, and epistemic location within the hegemonic Western framework. The noted Puerto Rican ethnic studies scholar Ramón Grosfoguel, for example, offers a clear and comprehensive summary of such postcolonial concerns: "Globalization studies, with a few exceptions, have not derived the epistemological and theoretical implications of the epistemic critique coming from subaltern locations in the colonial divide and expressed in academia through ethnic studies and woman studies. We still continue to produce a knowledge from the Western man 'point zero' god's-eye view."[29]

As we noted in previous chapters, most globalization theories deemed influential have been constructed in the Global North, which contains the powerful, capital-exporting countries of Europe, North America, and Australia/New Zealand. The principal architects of these theories are overwhelmingly white, male, and prosperous, even though processes of globalization disproportionally affect poor women and gender minorities of color in the Global South.[30] Mainstream globalization thinkers in the West tend to perceive and analyze relevant dynamics on the basis of theoretical models developed in and pertaining to their privileged regions. As we explored in chapter 1, some of the most significant globalization theories are centered on topics related to the global extension of Western modernity. To be sure, the European Enlightenment and the Industrial Revolution sparked social and scientific developments that proved to be crucial for the intensification of globalization. But a narrow focus on expanding features of Western modernity inevitably situates these global dynamics within the overarching Eurocentric systems of thought and practice that assume the superiority of Western knowledge systems. While promising universal knowledge, globalization narratives often neglect their historical embeddedness in a multiplicity of worldviews.

To add insult to injury, authoritative Northern globalization frameworks have been exported to the Global South. Over the past decades, this global transfer of knowledge has happened mostly indirectly through the education of Southern elites at prominent Northern universities. Conversely, alternative models fashioned by scores of intellectuals at the postcolonial periphery rarely receive a deserved exposure in the Euro-American academy. These structural imbalances reinforce the significance of power-knowledge dynamics in theorizing globalization. Hence, studying globalization processes requires an understanding of how organized power interests located in the economic and educational sectors of the Global North exert control over places and regions they habitually characterize as "less developed," "chaotic," or "rebellious."[31]

Over the last three decades, Walter Mignolo has emerged as a particularly influential globalization thinker. He applies his

> **Walter Mignolo (1941–)** is William H. Wannamaker Distinguished Professor of Romance Studies and Professor of Literature at Duke University, USA. The Argentinian-born scholar has published extensively on semiotics, literary theory, postcolonial theory, globalization theory, and global history. His sophisticated critical framework of globalization theory employs four innovative concepts to deconstruct/reconstruct the dominant model of Western modernity: globalism, the coloniality of power, the colonial matrix of power, and decoloniality. Mignolo has contributed to the founding of a special intellectual tradition: *the modernity/coloniality critical school of thought.*

critical lens to prevailing Eurocentric historical narratives that present the compression of world-space and world-time as a linear process originating in the supposedly superior social environment of the West. Mignolo's critical historical analysis, however, shows that important concepts, practices, technologies, and capacities were not simply diffused in unilinear fashion to the rest of the world. Rather, his work foregrounds multidirectional flows emanating from widely dispersed cultural centers and civilizations over long periods of time.

Moving from a critical scrutiny of Western historical narratives to equally discerning political and economic analyses of Eurocentrism, Mignolo argues that the supposedly neutral concepts *modernity* and *globalization* actually serve as ideological devices to naturalize and thus perpetuate the dominance of the Global North. In particular, these concepts function to suppress critical questions about who made and regulates globalization, who interprets and explains it, who changes and preserves it, and why and what for. Hence, Mignolo prefers the term *globalism* to signal that the latter is not merely an objective concept, but an *ideological* undertaking designed by neoliberal capitalist forces to promote what he calls the *coloniality of knowledge*. He notes that, since the sixteenth-century European capture of the "New World," such a narrow way of understanding the world has become hegemonic through the political enforcement of a *colonial matrix of power*. This term signifies a confluence of economic, political, and cultural-religious practices, which serves as a coercive device for ordering global social relations according to the interests of their Western designers.[32]

Mignolo adopts these crucial terms in his critical vocabulary from the writings of the late Peruvian sociologist Aníbal Quijano, known for his trenchant analysis of the contradictions between the glowing Enlightenment rhetoric of Western modernity and the implementation of colonial practices of dispossession, exploitation, and oppression. Developing and refining Quijano's model, Mignolo explains that *coloniality* also refers to the latest globalization phase of Western modernity. He anchors his critical understanding of globalization in a key passage of one of Quijano's essays, which deserves to be cited here in full:

> What is termed globalization is the culmination of a process that began with the constitution of America and colonial/modern Euro-centered capitalism as new global powers. One of the fundamental axes of this model of power is the social classification of the world's population around the idea of race, a mental construction that expresses the basic experience of colonial domination and pervades the more important dimensions of global power, including its specific rationality: Eurocentrism. The racial axis has a colonial

origin and character, but it has proven to be more durable and stable than the colonialism in whose matrix it was established.[33]

Likewise, Mignolo emphasizes that globalization is a racialized term that hides its constitutive second half: coloniality. Replacing it with the dual concept of *globalization/coloniality* helps to unmask this latest neoliberal iteration of the centuries-old project of Western *modernity/coloniality*. Most importantly, Mignolo argues that coloniality is not a feature of the past, but a social formation that survived the post–World War II political *decolonization process* only to be reassembled as the "underdeveloped" *Third World*. Hence, the coloniality of power continues as an oppressive constellation hiding behind the emancipatory promises of globalization. And the colonial matrix of power continues to secure the enduring Northern domination of all aspects of human experience in the Global South.[34]

But Mignolo's critique of globalization/coloniality as an ongoing project does not exhaust itself in such skilled deconstructive maneuvers. Switching to a constructive mode of critical thinking, he demands from globalization theorists the creation of alternative theoretical models of globalization without coloniality that can be utilized by postcolonial and indigenous movements around the world. Mignolo suggests that real emancipation from Northern domination can only come through a dual counterproject of *dewesternization* based on *multipolarity*, and *decoloniality* promoting *pluriversality*. Critical globalization theorists share a responsibility to create pluriversal and polycentric global future scenarios, which strip coloniality of its epistemological dominance. Anchored in decolonial ways of knowing, sensing, and imagining, such new visions challenge the principles, structure, and content of knowledges that hold together the colonial matrix of power. Mignolo describes his distinct critical style of theorizing globalization theory as "the advancement of decolonial thinking as a particular kind of critical theory and to the decolonial option as a specific orientation of doing."[35]

CONCLUDING CRITICAL REFLECTIONS

Critical globalization thinkers—whether located inside or outside the field—provide an invaluable service to globalization theory by revealing its weaknesses and provoking better responses. Stage 1–focused critics like Rosenberg and, to a lesser extent, Hirst/Thompson contribute to the evolution of globalization theory by questioning the logics and the evidence base of its theoretical arguments. They identify problems such as imprecise definitions, the failure to specify indicators of quantifiable measurements, and difficulties of generating hypotheses capable of being set against empirical evidence.[36]

They also offer thoughtful objections to the efforts made by generalizing globalization thinkers to develop an overarching conceptual framework of explaining social change across the domains of the entire global system. Bristling at these ambitious attempts to resurrect twentieth-century grand theory as twenty-first-century globalization theory, Stage 1 critics deny that there exists a single, totalizing framework of global interconnectedness, which can serve as the background condition for all social life on this planet.[37] At the same time, however, by confining their mode of theorizing to analytical critical thinking, Stage 1 theorists neglect their ethical responsibility to expose the concrete harms caused by particular forms of globalization and thus contribute to the improvement of the lives of sentient beings on this planet.

Stepping into this normative gap, Stage 2 thinkers committed to global justice, indigeneity, decoloniality, and other ways of improving the quality of life on our planet utilize their critical style of inquiry to make visible the many biases and positions of privilege that are part of the dominant framework of globalization theory. Hence, socially engaged perspectives have the virtue of confronting globalization theory with ethical questions that are often relegated to the margins of social-scientific inquiries. Is globalization less of a transnational process and more of a colonial project? Is globalization theory sufficiently global to represent the diverse voices of the multitude and speak to the diverse experiences of disempowered people around the world? What sort of new and innovative ideas have been produced by public intellectuals who do not necessarily travel along the theoretical and geographical paths frequented by mainstream globalization thinkers? What are the most pressing issues and promising intellectual approaches that have been neglected?

Some of these questions also shine a critical spotlight on the hegemonic role of the English language in globalization theory. With English still expanding its status as the academic lingua franca, thinkers embedded in Western universities still hold the monopoly on the production of globalization theories. Important contributions from the Global South in languages other than English often fall through the cracks or register only in translated form on the radar of the supposedly global academic publishing network years after their original publication. In the last few decades, the United States, the United Kingdom, Canada, and Australia have served as powerful economic magnets for English-speaking academics from the Global South while also posing as the obvious hegemonic target of their criticisms. On one hand, this influx of non-Western academics has resulted

166 / *Critical Theories*

in the more effective production and worldwide dissemination of their critical English-language publications. On the other, however, the resulting brain drain not only amplifies the intellectual disadvantage of the Global South, but also exacerbates the academic marginalization of most languages on this planet.

One serious problem plaguing Stage 2 globalization thinkers is that they sometimes lose themselves in ideological polemics that ride roughshod over the Stage 1 ideal of balanced assessment. It is one thing to express righteous anger at the many abuses of prevailing global practices linked to unequal power relations that still govern our world. Yet, it is quite another to let the furies of resentment eclipse one's critical normative reflexivity. A dogmatic retreat into fixed identity positions at the expense of articulating a transcultural global vision does not seem to be a satisfying alternative either. As Jan Aart Scholte points out, perhaps the most valuable goal for *all* critical globalization thinkers should be the elaboration of a cross-cultural ethical framework based on a number of core principles. These include: deep reflexivity on the part of everyone in the global encounter; high sensitivity to knowledge/ power relations; proper recognition of cultural complexity; a committed default position of embracing diversity; humility in the face of challenging and perhaps unpalatable differences; deep listening to otherness; and a willingness to learn for mutual change.[38]

Still, it seems that normatively balanced forms of Stage 2 critical thinking have yet to make more headway in globalization theory. Our discussion of the developing links between critical globalization theory and emancipatory social movements should not seduce us into assuming that most globalization thinkers support radical or even moderate socially engaged perspectives. An informal perusal of influential globalization literature produced during the last fifteen years suggests that nearly all authors express some appreciation for Stage 1 critical thinking as a cognitive ability to see the multiple sides of globalization. However, less than half of these globalization theorists take their understanding of "critical" to the normative Stage 2 of critical thinking that actively challenges dominant social arrangements and promotes emancipatory social change. This means that there is plenty of room for improvement.

Let us close this chapter with one more virtue of the critical mode of theorizing globalization: it easily combines with the other three styles of inquiry discussed in this book. Generalizing theorists like David Held use critical thinking in their construction of a comprehensive globalization framework that should guide transformative social change. Domain theorists like William Robinson and Jan Nederveen Pieterse employ it to criticize global capitalism and endorse symbolic forms and identities that give rise to a global mélange. Complexity theorists like Saskia Sassen embrace it as a way to highlight the injustice of intricate practices of systemic expulsions that drive poor and marginal people from spatial zones of privilege. On the flipside, however, the remarkable flexibility and adaptability of the critical mode is countered by the fact that it can hardly stand on its own. After all, to engage in criticism always means to criticize *something*—an object, subject, process, institution, structure, and so on. In the case of globalization theory, the power of the critical style only comes to full life as it joins forces with the other modes of theorizing discussed in this book.

NOTES

1. Daniel T. Willingham, "Critical Thinking: Why Is It So Hard to Teach?," *American Educator*, Summer 2007, 8.

168 / *Critical Theories*

2. Pierre Bourdieu, "For a Scholarship with Commitment," in *Firing Back: Against the Tyranny of the Market 2* (New York: The New Press, 2002), 24–25.

3. See Stephen Eric Bronner, *Critical Theory: A Very Short Introduction* (Oxford, UK: Oxford University Press, 2011), 7.

4. For a book-length discussion of various forms of "globaloney," see Michael Veseth, *Globaloney 2.0: The Crash of 2008 and the Future of Globalization* (Lanham, MD: Rowman & Littlefield, 2010).

5. Justin Rosenberg, *The Follies of Globalisation Theory* (London: Verso, 2000); see also Rosenberg, "Globalization Theory: A Post Mortem," *International Politics* 42 (2005): 2–74; and Rosenberg, "And the Definition of Globalisation Is? ... A Reply to 'In at the Death' by Barrie Axford," *Globalizations* 4, no. 3 (2007): 417–21.

6. Susan Strange, *The Retreat of the State: The Diffusion of Power in the World Economy* (Cambridge, UK: Cambridge University Press, 1996), xii–xiii. See also Linda Weiss, *The Myth of the Powerless State: Governing the Economy in a Global Era* (Ithaca, NY: Cornell University Press, 1998), 212.

7. Rosenberg, "And the Definition of Globalisation Is?," 418–19.

8. Rosenberg, 420.

9. Rosenberg, "Globalization Theory," 3, 66.

10. For insightful summaries of Rosenberg's critique of globalization theory and possible retorts, see Barrie Axford, "In at the Death? Reflections on Justin Rosenberg's 'Post-Mortem' on Globalization," *Globalizations* 4, no. 2 (2007): 171–91; and Andrew Jones, *Globalization: Key Thinkers* (Cambridge, UK: Polity Press, 2010), 46–50.

11. See, for example, Manfred B. Steger, *Globalization: A Very Short Introduction* (Oxford, UK: Oxford University Press, 2003), 7–9; Martin Albrow, *The Global Age* (Stanford, CA: Stanford University Press, 1997), 4–6, 80–89; David Held, Anthony McGrew, David Goldblatt, and Jonathan Perraton, eds., *Global Transformations* (Cambridge, UK: Polity Press, 1999), 1–31; and James H. Mittelman, *The Globalization Syndrome: Transformation and Resistance* (Princeton, NJ: Princeton University Press, 2000), 4.

12. Paul Hirst and Grahame Thompson, *Globalization in Question: The International Economy and the Possibilities of Governance*, 2nd ed. (Cambridge: Polity Press, 1999), 2.

13. See Luc Boltanski, *On Critique: A Sociology of Emancipation* (Cambridge, UK: Polity Press, 2011), 1–5.

14. For a discussion of the method of "thick description," see Clifford Geertz, *The Interpretation of Cultures*, 3rd ed. (New York: Basic Books, 2017), 3–36.

15. See Manfred B. Steger, James Goodman, and Erin K. Wilson, *Justice Globalism: Ideology, Crises, Policy* (London: Sage Publications, 2013).

16. Richard P. Appelbaum and William I. Robinson, eds., *Critical Globalization Studies* (New York: Routledge, 2005). See also Chamsy El-Ojeili and Patrick Hayden, eds., *Critical Theories of Globalization: An Introduction* (Houndmills, UK: Palgrave Macmillan, 2006).

17. William I. Robinson, "What Is a Critical Globalization Studies? Intellectual Labor and Global Society," in Appelbaum and Robinson, *Critical Globalization Studies*, 14–17.

18. Richard Appelbaum and William I. Robinson, "Introduction," in Appelbaum and Robinson, *Critical Globalization Studies*, xii–xiii.

19. James H. Mittelman, *Whither Globalization: The Vortex of Knowledge and Ideology* (London: Routledge, 2004), 40–1, 98.

20. See Hans Schattle, *Globalization & Citizenship* (Lanham, MD: Rowman & Littlefield Publishers, 2012).

21. Mittelman, *Whither Globalization?*, 44–45.

22. Mark Juergensmeyer, "What Is Global Studies," *global-e: A Global Studies Journal* 5 (2012), http://global-ejournal.org/2011/05/06/what-is-global-studies-3/.

23. Mittelman, "What Is a Critical Globalization Studies?," 24–25.

24. Edward Said, *Orientalism* (New York: Vintage, 1979).

25. Robert J.C. Young, *Postcolonialism: A Very Short Introduction* (Oxford, UK: Oxford University Press, 2003), 6–7.

26. Dana Hickey, "Indigenous Epistemologies, Worldviews, and Theories of Power," *Turtle Island Journal of Indigenous Health* 1, no. 1 (2020): 14–25.

27. Boaventura de Souza Santos, *Epistemologies of the South: Justice against Epistemicide* (Boulder, CO: Paradigm Publishers, 2014), 92.

28. See, for example, Sankaran Krishna, *Globalization & Postcolonialism: Hegemony and Resistance in the Twenty-first Century* (Lanham, MD; Rowman & Littlefield, 2009).

170 / *Critical Theories*

29. Ramón Grosfoguel, "The Implications of Subaltern Epistemologies for Global Capitalism: Transmodernity, Border Thinking, and Global Coloniality," in Appelbaum and Robinson, *Critical Globalization Studies*, 284.

30. Raewyn Connell, *Southern Theory: The Global Dynamics of Knowledge in Social Science* (Crow's Nest, New South Wales: Allen & Unwin, 2007), vii; Gül Çaliskan and Kayla Preston, "Introduction," in Gül Çaliskan, ed., *Gendering Globalization, Globalizing Gender: Postcolonial Perspectives* (Don Mills, ON: Oxford University Press Canada, 2020), x.

31. Arjun Appadurai, "The Production of Locality," in Richard Fardon, ed., *Counterworks: Managing the Diversity of Knowledge* (Minneapolis: University of Minnesota, 1995), 208–29; Ugo Dessi and Franciscu Sedda, "Glocalization and Everyday Life," *Glocalism: A Journal for Culture, Politics, and Innovation* 3 (2020), https://doi.org/10.12893/gjcpi.2020.3.14.

32. Walter Mignolo, "The Explosion of Globalism and the Advent of the Third Nomos of the Earth," in Manfred B. Steger, Roland Benedikter, Harald Pechlaner, and Ingrid Kofler, eds., *Globalization: Past, Present, Future* (Berkeley: University of California Press, 2023), 194–95.

33. Aníbal Quijano, "Coloniality of Power, Eurocentrism and Social Classification," in Mabel Moraña, Enrique Dussel, and Carlos A. Jáuregui, eds., *Coloniality at Large: Latin America and the Postcolonial Debate* (Durham, NC: Duke University Press, 2008), 181.

34. Walter Mignolo, "Coloniality and Globalization: A Decolonial Take," *Globalizations* 18, no. 5 (2021): 729–30.

35. Walter Mignolo, "Introduction: Coloniality of Power and Decolonial Thinking," in Walter Mignolo and Arturo Escobar, eds., *Globalization and the Decolonial Question* (London: Routledge, 2010), 1.

36. See also Axford, *Theories of Globalization*, 188.

37. James H. Mittelman, "What's in a Name? Global, International, and Regional Studies," *Globalizations* 10, no. 4 (2013): 516.

38. Jan Aart Scholte, "Whither Global Theory?," *Protosociology* 33 (2016): 219.

CHAPTER FIVE

New Theories

Our concise introduction to globalization theories is drawing to a close. In the previous chapters, we linked our exploration of the four modes of theorizing to theories developed in response to globalization processes that unfolded in the 1990s and 2000s. After all, these earlier approaches laid the conceptual foundation for what became the transdisciplinary field of global studies. However, our overview of globalization theories would remain incomplete without a consideration of more recent contributions that emerged in interaction with the altered globalization dynamics of the last fifteen years as a result of the intensification of *global problems* such as the instability and volatility of financial markets, the growing impact of digital technology, the surge of right-wing national populism, the rapid spread of deadly pandemics, rising geopolitical tensions, and the mounting ecological challenges threatening the survival of many species in our geological age of the *Anthropocene*. A comprehensive account of these more recent developments would transcend the scope of this book, but this chapter can nonetheless provide a selective overview of three innovative theoretical models that have surfaced in recent years: deglobalization theories, disjunctive globalization theories, and ecological globalization theories.

The first section in this chapter starts with an examination of *deglobalization theories*, which have been popular ever since the 2008 Global Financial Crisis. The ensuing era of the *Great Unsettling* has led some pessimistic political economists to issue blanket statements that globalization-in-general is waning. However, more nuanced perspectives suggest that globalization is far from suffering a complete breakdown. Hence, the debate over the alleged retreat of globalization is tied to the rigidity of domain thinking, which reduces the compression of world-space and world-time to *economic* processes such as global trade and investment flows. We explore the contending theoretical frameworks of deglobalization through the helpful classification scheme introduced by the Turkish social thinker Didem Buhari. The section closes with a brief consideration of alternative interpretations of deglobalization as *reglobalization*.

Next, we turn to a special group of reglobalization theorists who utilize the complexity mode of inquiry to assemble what they call *disjunctive globalization theory*. As an influential example of this approach, we consider Paul James and Manfred Steger's typology featuring four major globalization formations, which frame their critical examination of structural disjunctures and fissures straining the global system. James and Steger point to the rapid advancement of digital technology—captured by the trendy term *digitization*—as a major contributor to the intensification of disjointed globalization dynamics first noticed by the social anthropologist Arjun Appadurai more than three decades ago. They also assert that these widening cleavages occurring at the macro level also reach deeply into the micro layer of subjective consciousness to produce an *unhappy consciousness* torn between the enjoyment of the flexible disembodiment in cyberspace and the embodied attachment to local lifeworlds.

As the third example of new globalization theories, the next section discusses emerging ecological perspectives. We focus especially on Eve Darian-Smith's constructive critique of "blinkered globalization theory" as not only neglecting crucial environmental issues but remaining overly attached to the modernist Euro-American paradigm. Her alternative framework of a *climate-driven globalization theory* builds on the concrete examples of catastrophic wildfires sweeping across the planet to bring into a productive conversation seemingly unrelated issues of ecological devastation, racism, extractivist capitalism, and biased, Western-centric worldviews that are often discussed in isolation from each other.

We end our overview and discussion with the briefest of speculations about how globalization theories might be evolving in the near future.

DEGLOBALIZATION THEORIES

The term *deglobalization* has been used for some time to refer to various social processes stalling, or even reversing, the transnational flows of people, ideas, things, and institutions that have been swelling since the rise of neoliberal capitalism in the late twentieth century. Many commentators have placed the concept squarely within the economic domain to signify the alleged disintegration of global trade and investment. Deglobalization dynamics tend to be measured mostly by various economic indicators such as transnational commerce flows, foreign direct investment, and the presence of tariff barriers to international trade. For this reason, the meaning of deglobalization is strongly linked to the concept of *economic nationalism*, which refers to a mode of governance that favors strong state action to create, bolster, and protect national economies.[1] In recent years, the term has gained much currency among globalization theorists as a result of four disruptive global events they hold responsible for what they interpret as a retreat of globalization.

First, the 2008 Global Financial Crisis not only brought global capitalism to the verge of collapse, but also triggered the Great Recession as well as the ensuing Eurozone Sovereign Debt Crisis of the 2010s. These epic economic meltdowns of global proportions shattered the previous confidence in the worldwide integration of finance, trade, and governance. They also affected a profound shift in the public mood away from the dominant market-globalist ideology, which was actively propagated by U.S. governments and key international economic institutions. As the neoliberal globalization system was losing its luster in the Global North, select regions in China and other parts of Asia continued to benefit from their advantageous position of low-wage suppliers in the global economy.

Second, the threats to corporate globalization grew even more intense when nationalist-populist forces capitalized on the rising negative perception of deregulated markets. During the 2010s, globalization became *the* political punching bag for resurgent nationalism around the world. Promising a return to domestic control, national populists like Donald Trump, Viktor Orbán, and Jair Bolsonaro denounced globalization even though their political rise owed much to their adroit use of global digital communication technology such as Twitter and Facebook in shaping public opinion in cyberspace. The ensuing shift in voter behavior toward the political right was reflected not only in the stunning electoral triumphs of Trumpism in the United States and Brexit in the United Kingdom, but also in the reversal of the decades-long global advance of democracy as illiberal forces made gains in many parts of the world.

Third, the early 2020s saw the COVID-19 pandemic sweeping across the planet, uprooting the lives of its nearly 8 billion human inhabitants. By 2024, official numbers showed that 775 million people had contracted multiple variants of the disease, resulting in at least 7 million confirmed deaths. Existing global interdependencies and mobilities ran up against major pandemic-related obstacles caused by repeated national lockdowns, severe travel restrictions, extended travel quarantines, strict social distancing rules, a noticeable shift to working-from-home, and enduring global supply-chain interruptions. For globalization scholars, this once-in-a-century health crisis proved to be an especially challenging factor, since it required the building of broad multidisciplinary research frameworks leading to a better understanding of its complex impacts on the major domains of globalization.

Fourth, geopolitical competition among the Great Powers was increasing in the 2010s and 2020s. And, China, Russia, and India continued to challenge U.S. world leadership on multiple fronts. The Russian annexation of the Crimean Peninsula in 2014, China's forward posture in the South China Sea, plus its political crackdown on Hong Kong, and the ongoing tensions on the Korean peninsula marked this new era of geopolitical conflict. Mounting hostility came to a head in 2022 with Russia's full-blown invasion of Ukraine, with a protracted war ensuing. This major act of aggression was met with the imposition of unprecedented economic sanctions levied by a U.S.-led broad coalition of countries against the Russian Federation. Finally,

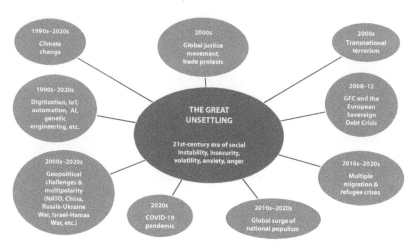

Figure 17. The Great Unsettling

the outbreak of the Israel-Hamas War in October 2023 added more fuel to the geopolitical conflagrations around the world. For the first time since the end of the Cold War, a global nuclear confrontation appeared to be a distinct possibility.

The magnitude of these four global crises unfolding alongside existing problems such as escalating climate change and soaring levels of economic inequality within countries suggested to many experts that globalization was in real trouble. In particular, the disruption of everyday life caused by the novel coronavirus underlined our present era as one characterized by a *Great Unsettling*—shorthand for the intensifying global dynamics of dislocation, insecurity, and volatility.[2] Globalization thinkers who saw the Great Unsettling as part of the larger process of deglobalization began to assemble theoretical frameworks around their key concept. Didem Buhari's recent overview of these classification schemes identifies three distinct theoretical approaches to deglobalization.[3]

New Theories / 177

> **Didem Buhari (1981–)** is Associate Professor of International Relations at Izmir Katip Celebi University, Türkiye (formerly Turkey). She was previously a postdoctoral research fellow at the London School of Economics, Oxford Brookes University, and taught at various universities in the United Kingdom. Her main areas of academic expertise include globalization theory, international relations theory, and Türkiye's social and political relations with the West. Assessing the main theoretical approaches to deglobalization, Buhari concludes that equating the meaning of this concept to the alleged end of globalization in the twenty-first century is oversimplistic. In her view, such a perspective neglects the complexities and multidimensionality of global interconnectivities and mobilities.

According to Buhari, the first account is represented by thinkers who define deglobalization as, simply, the *reverse* or *opposite of globalization* as measured by its allegedly diminishing component parts. They tend to focus on the economic and political domains such as trade, foreign direct investment, and lagging global governance structures. As we noted at the outset of this section, this rather pessimistic perspective predicts an end to globalization as the intensification of global crises forces nation-states to turn inward. In other words, strengthening deglobalization dynamics correspond to active efforts by national governments to return to territoriality, sovereignty, and economic self-sufficiency. Accordingly, thinkers belonging in this category present deglobalization as an economic phenomenon that has sparked state-initiated measures toward a less connected world.

178 / *New Theories*

In fact, they appreciate *moderate* forms of deglobalization as a useful development with the potential of strengthening democratic forms of decentralization and localization. As we are entering a new era of localization, economic and political activity is being refocused toward finding local solutions to social problems rather than simply handing control to global free-market institutions.[4] Another variation in this first account in Buhari's overview portrays deglobalization as a necessary contestation of the U.S.-led liberal global order by the rising powers in the non-Western world led by China, Russia, and India. While some thinkers fear that deglobalization represents a long-lasting structural phenomenon undermining economic growth, this group welcomes it as a temporary phenomenon that weakens Western capitalist hegemony.[5]

The postcolonial flavor inherent in this variant is significantly amplified in what Buhari identifies as the second account of deglobalization. Presented as the *re-empowerment of the local and national*, this defiant perspective on deglobalization was pioneered by the Filipino sociologist Walden Bello in the early 2000s. Since then, it has attracted a large following among thinkers in the Global South as well as sympathetic Northern theorists.[6] At the core of this perspective lies the demand for a wholesale *delinking* from the corporate elite–driven globalization system. These deglobalization thinkers contend, however, that this desired rupture should be only temporary and followed by alternative projects designed to build a voluntary global network of local communities committed to participatory democracy and need-based economic systems. This means that such a bottom-up project of breaking with global capitalism and political centralization would not abandon the globalist vision of worldwide interconnectivities. But it would mandate that the process must start at the local level and preserve people-centered arrangements in the service of local needs. Such ideas about delinking from the global economy without repudiating capitalist modes of production have also been articulated on the political right. But they entail the fundamental demolition of all forms of globalization through comprehensive policies of de-internationalization initiated by nation-states.[7] On both ends of the ideological spectrum, then, the ultimate goal of deglobalization understood as *localization* is the reduction of existing economic and political dependencies on external forces.

Buhari refers to the third approach as the *waves of deglobalization* model. This perspective is delivered in the domain style of theorizing globalization and focuses on economic processes: throughout history, periods of hyperglobalization have been followed by counterphases of deglobalization. For example, the long globalization wave from the 1870s to the 1910s dissipated in the upheavals of World War I and the Great Depression. The ensuing deglobalization backlash took the political form of the extreme nationalist movements of the 1930s, which promised to shelter citizens from the negative consequences of unfettered capitalism. Hence, proponents of the waves of deglobalization model suggest that each globalization wave carries its own seeds of destruction by generating political forces opposed to internationalization. Their goal is to correct the social problems caused by economic globalization—mostly in the form of growing inequality and job losses—by imposing protective economic policies and cultural measures such as trade tariffs, foreign investment controls, and immigration restrictions. In short, rather than being merely the opposite of globalization, deglobalization thinkers in this category theorize globalization as inextricably linked to wax-and-wane phases of the world economy. But the thrust of their thinking is ultimately directed at solving practical problems. Analyzing deglobalization within the waves model may help build the knowledge necessary to design global policies aimed at the reduction of extremes on both ends of the (de)globalization cycles.[8]

Buhari's meticulous overview of deglobalization theories organizes the proliferating literature on the subject around these three theoretical accounts. However, she only hints at what might be considered a fourth, and perhaps most promising, emerging academic perspective: *deglobalization* understood as *reglobalization*. Such a seemingly contradictory approach starts with the recognition that deglobalization cannot be essentialized as diminishing global interdependence. As many historical examples demonstrate, connective and disconnective processes are deeply interwoven. Separating them in--a binary fashion--eclipses more than it illuminates. Unlike the proponents of the waves model, reglobalization thinkers also reject the proposition that integrative and disintegrative dynamics simply follow each other like pendulum swings. Rather, they interpret connectivity and rupture as turbulent and multilayered movements that incessantly interact with each other in productive ways. Hence, they consider the inherent tensions and interplays between these opposing forces as the engine of open-ended globalization processes resulting in constant social reconstruction.[9]

Utilizing a complexity style of inquiry, reglobalization thinkers envision deglobalization as neither a linear nor an accumulative dynamic, but as an intricate *emergent process* establishing connections as well as producing breaks, delays, and absences in various forms and intensities. They admonish globalization theorists to examine more seriously the *constructive* roles of ruptures in the forging of new global interdependencies. In their view, analyzing disconnection in this manner also leads to a broader understanding of the Great Unsettling. Global crises, in particular, should be interpreted as more than discrete moments of disruption and dislocation. They also constitute periods of opportunity that harbor creative potentials for restructuring social relations across world-space and world-time. As Roland Benedikter, one of the world's leading theorists of reglobalization, emphasizes, reglobalization should be acknowledged as a *key concept* in globalization theory because it expands our understanding of the extent to which globalization is being reconfigured by a combination of integrative and disintegrative shifts, events, and forces. For Benedikter, designing new theoretical models of reglobalization is a crucial task that should not only appeal to academics but also attract policy-makers eager to find practical solutions to pressing global problems.[10]

DISJUNCTIVE GLOBALIZATION THEORIES

Reglobalization perspectives possess the additional virtue of broadening the narrow economic focus that confines the imagination of many deglobalization proponents. Rather than reducing globalization to a monolithic process of growing worldwide economic interconnectivity, reglobalization thinkers emphasize the multidimensionality of the phenomenon. As a result, they foreground the complexity of mixed (dis)integration processes, which can be traced to distinct globalization formations operating at different speeds and intensities. Some theorists who initially started as reglobalization proponents have extended their thinking to create an innovative conceptual framework dedicated to the exploration of globalization's increasingly *disjointed* movements and trajectories in the twenty-first century.

The construction of such *disjunctive globalization theories* usually starts with the difficult task of creating new globalization typologies that better capture the multiplicity and complexity of global flows. The social anthropologist Arjun Appadurai was the first globalization thinker to develop such an improved classification scheme in the early 1990s. Tracing the movement of significant disjunctures between economic, cultural, and political flows with the help of the complexity and generalizing style of inquiry, Appadurai argues that globalization occurs in five realms or *scapes* created by global economic and cultural flows. These distinct contexts include *ethnoscapes* (shifting populations made up of tourists, immigrants, refugees, and exiles); *technoscapes* (development of technologies that facilitate the rise of TNCs); *finanscapes* (flows of global capital); *mediascapes* (electronic communication capabilities to produce and disseminate information); and *ideoscapes* (ideologies produced by governments, corporations, and social movements).

Acknowledging that globalization throughout human history has always been characterized by disjointed flows of people, ideas, and objects, Appadurai nonetheless argues that these dynamics have been greatly accelerated in the late twentieth century. As a result, we have been witnessing the production of new social imaginaries that allow individuals and groups around the world to make sense of their expanded social existence in these multiple scapes. The recognition of the significance of changing forms of human consciousness brought on by disjointed global flows allows Appadurai to highlight the urgency of studying in far more detail the subjective forms of globalization that tend to be neglected by economic domain thinkers. Moreover, his disjunctive model of globalization is built on the rejection of binaries and dualisms that have plagued globaliza-

New Theories / 183

Paul James (1958-) is Professor of Globalization and Cultural Diversity at Western Sydney University. He also served as the scientific advisor to the mayor of Berlin, as well as the director of the UN Global Compact Cities Programme. His numerous publications span the fields of globalization theory, social theory, political theory, cultural studies, urban studies, social anthropology, and indigenous studies. James's major contribution to globalization theory is reflected in his astute exploration of the changing configurations of globalization by combining three modes of theorizing: complexity, critical, and generalizing. Most importantly, he developed with Manfred B. Steger what they call an *engaged theory of globalization*, which opens the way to spatially and historically specific explanations within a recognition of broader structures of social relations.

tion theory such as the quarrel over cultural sameness or differentiation we discussed in chapter 2.[11]

Building on Appadurai's presentation of globalization as a set of complex and disjointed processes, Paul James and Manfred B. Steger also question some of its assumptions. In particular, they object to Appadurai's five-scape classification scheme as reinforcing simplistic domain divisions among economics, politics, and culture that are increasingly challenged by new globalization dynamics that cut across these dimensions. Instead, they introduce their innovative theoretical model based on *four social formations of globalization*. In their view, this typology is better equipped to capture the growing significance of disjunctive globalization dynamics.

184 / New Theories

James and Steger refer to the first social formation as *embodied globalization*, which encompasses the worldwide interconnectivities and mobilities of people, including tourists, refugees, business travelers, and so on. Second, *disembodied globalization* relates to worldwide interconnectivities and mobilities of increasingly digitized ideas, information, images, and data. Third, *objectified globalization* involves worldwide interconnectivities and mobilities of things, ranging from tradable commodities transported around the world by gigantic container ships to the molecular components of greenhouse gases. Finally, *institutional globalization* refers to worldwide interconnections and mobilities of organizations, including TNCs, international economic institutions like the IMF and the WTO, legal institutions like the International Court of Justice, and global sports clubs such as Real Madrid and the New York Yankees.

Having identified these four globalization formations, James and Steger liken them to moving tectonic plates whose complex dynamics have shaped the geology of our planet in profound ways. Possessing both an underlying structure—a *formation*—and a visible morphology or shape—a *form*—both geological and globalization dynamics are bonded by substantial synergies as well as driven apart by potent antagonisms. In the contemporary period of the Great Unsettling, the movements of the four globalization formations have become increasingly desynchronized and disjointed. James and Steger suggest that the most consequential disjuncture destabilizing the current global system has been occurring between its increasingly *digitized*, disembodied formation and the other three configurations. In short, it is the growing *digitization* affecting all aspects of everyday life that drives disjunctive globalization.[12]

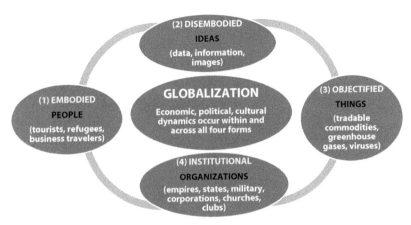

Figure 18. Paul James and Manfred Steger's four globalization formations

Digitization refers to a set of rapidly unfolding processes that originally started with micro- and network-computing in the second half of the twentieth century. But it hardly stopped there. Proliferating electronic technologies based on a series of electronic binary digits known as *bits* have been operating in the everyday lives of billions of people, in the process transforming nearly all aspects of social relations.[13] Global flows of data primarily consist of information, searches, communications, transactions of all kinds, video, streaming, gaming, and so on. James and Steger note that the datasphere has been growing by about 18 million gigabytes per minute, aided by digital technologies capable of capturing and processing human behavioral information at an unprecedented speed and volume. Commercial enterprises from large corporations like Amazon and Alibaba to small and medium-sized enterprises increasingly turn to digital platforms to connect to customers and suppliers across national borders. In addition, small start-up companies can become global in a heartbeat by exploiting digital platforms.[14]

The global digital leap pertains to everything some social thinkers associate with the *Fourth Industrial Revolution*. Its major technological innovations include Big Data and augmented analytics that enable the integration of digital information through automated mining, harvesting, tagging, linking, and archiving of data; the expansion of bandwidth that allows for the emergence of 5G networks; quantum computing that operates far more quickly than the fastest processors available only a few years ago; digital platforms that infuse day-to-day disembodied social practices and engagements; the Internet of Things (IoT) and advanced smart devices that provide worldwide online connections among billions of everyday devices and objects; blockchain technologies like Bitcoin and other cryptocurrencies that allow multiple parties to engage in secure digital transactions without intermediaries; digitally extended realities; AI and digital machine learning capable of making decisions, carrying out tasks, and even predicting future outcomes based on what they process from data; robotics and drones that respond to their environment and perform routine or complex tasks autonomously; and nanotechnology that manipulates and controls matter at the atomic and molecular levels. These digital systems and practices run on complex algorithms, which are programable series of logical steps that organize and act upon data to achieve specific outcomes.[15]

As James and Steger point out, the thickening global network society of the twenty-first century shows high levels of interdependence, but it also nurtures widening rifts that threaten its systemic integrity. As measured according to David Held's criteria of extensity, intensity, velocity, and impact, *digital globaliza-*

tion has been charging ahead while the embodied, objectified, and institutional formations are lagging behind. As the mobility of people, things, and institutions fails to keep up with swelling digital flows, the growing stature of the disembodied globalization system begins to devour ever-larger pieces of its adjacent formations. For example, the application of 3D printing has been transforming the global merchandise trade built on global value chains—an important aspect of objectified globalization—into regionalized and localized networks of exchange based on digitally enabled production-on-demand facilities located as close to the end market as possible.

James and Steger fear that the digital disjuncture driving apart the four major globalization formations is likely to intensify with the ongoing inventions of new digital technologies that are being scaled at an ever-faster pace while decreasing rapidly in price. Indeed, digital technologies are so-called *exponential technologies*, which means that they develop, not in linear fashion, but at an accelerating pace of more than 10 percent per year for several decades. Consider, for example, TikTok, the Chinese-owned social network for sharing videos. In a matter of months, it went from a virtually unknown digital service to the most downloaded app in the world.[16]

Other disjunctive globalization thinkers like Richard Baldwin refer to the ongoing digital transformation of previously objectified and embodied forms of transnational interconnectivity as the coming *globotics upheaval* impacting the manufacturing sector by eliminating millions of embodied jobs and threatening to overwhelm the human capacity to adapt. Even the service sector is allegedly being cannibalized by disembodied globalization's growing ability to transform embodied workers thousands of miles away into digital tele-migrants by means of

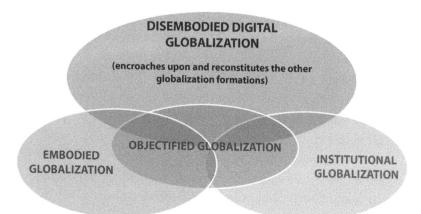

Figure 19. Disjunctive globalization: Extensity

collaborative software packages. In short, the disjunctures created by accelerating digital globalization have resulted in social disintegration and the growth of unaccountable power.[17]

Indeed, theoretical models of disjunctive globalization open up new perspectives on power dynamics in our global network society. Digital technologies are not neutral tools applied by detached human users, but artifacts built by people under specific social-economic conditions that reflect inherent asymmetrical power relations. The application of a critical style of thinking to analyze intensifying digital globalization brings into sharper focus novel forms of intangible power. The goal of those corporate interests wielding this power is to control and exploit human behavior across national borders by encoding digital technology into global infrastructures that remain opaque and unaccountable to ordinary citizens.

This power dimension linked to digitization has been the subject of new globalization theories that criticize the exploitative practices of TNCs like Google, Meta/Facebook, and Amazon. Their reliance on digitization has created new forms of *surveillance capitalism* or *platform capitalism*. Big Tech has been seeking to claim everyday human experience as free material for translation into behavioral data designed to fuel and shape human beings toward profitable outcomes. The prospect of a datafied lifeworld dominated by ever more authoritarian corporate surveillance infrastructures draws attention to the *posthuman* features of a new global cultural economy. Its digital communication technologies are designed to produce an indifferent globality of machines dependent on the hidden agency of algorithms. Such digital exploitation practices strip away the illusion that networked globalization formations retain some moral content, that being connected on the web is somehow intrinsically prosocial, innately inclusive, or naturally tending toward the democratization of knowledge. Rather, as these critics of digital globalization point out, online connectivity can be made to serve political forms of authoritarianism and limitless commercial profit.[18]

James and Steger concur that dominance of disembodied global relations cuts across all social domains and potentially benefits authoritarian forces. Moreover, the all-encompassing disjunctive globalization dynamics also reach deeply into the subjective aspects of personhood. As a result of their ever-expanding exposure to cyberspace and digital instantaneity, people experience a sense of dislocation and alienation from the local as manifested in conventional embodied, objectified, and institutionalized places. Their newly perceived sluggishness of the local compares unfavorably with the thrills of digital mobility and plasticity. Hence, the growing disjuncture between people's experiences of intensifying global interconnectivity in virtual reality and their existence in the more slowly moving globalization spheres leads to the creation of what James and Steger call an *unhappy consciousness*. Unhappiness manifests in the form of a *divided self*, torn between its desire for the pleasures of digital mobility and its visceral affection for embodied social relations. Hence, their analysis of disjunctive globalization makes for a better understanding of how, precisely, objective dynamics at the macro level interact with the subjective sphere of individual consciousness to produce new forms of alienation and anxiety in our era of the Great Unsettling.[19]

Most disjunctive globalization thinkers argue that the 2020–23 coronavirus pandemic has further accelerated and intensified the systemic dynamics of disjunctive globalization that were already underway prior to the outbreak. COVID-19 represented a fundamental inflection point that slowed embodied and objectified globalization while extending the reach of digital technology into people's everyday lives in the twenty-first century through the growth of the digital platform economy. For many months, most national borders were closed to migrants and travelers other than citizens returning home. Physical mobility was curtailed even within the nation-state. *Social distancing* became a ubiquitous global term referring to a government-mandated practice of physical dispersion while instances of distant socializing via digital platforms like Zoom exploded. Similarly, social media platforms like Facebook, Twitter, LinkedIn, and Snapchat experienced enormous increases that have continued beyond the peak pandemic years.[20]

Even when the WHO announced in 2023 that COVID-19 no longer qualified as a global health emergency, neither the pace of disjunctive globalization had slowed down nor had the pandemic-intensified social dynamics faded away. People around the world continued to look to digital media sites of all kinds to cultivate disembodied connections to supplement the waning physical experiences. A good deal of scientific evidence shows that extended time spent online produces new patterns of everyday consciousness, many of which are detrimental to mental health. Indeed, recent medical studies have established a conclusive link between COVID-19-intensified social media use and an increased risk of mental health issues such as internalizing problems—social withdrawal, difficulty coping with anxiety or depression, or directing feelings inward—and externalizing issues—aggression, acting out, and violence, especially among young adults.[21]

However, most disjunctive globalization theorists also acknowledge that the acceleration of digital globalization has *positive impacts* as well. People with particular disabilities, for example, rely on the cybersphere for social contact. During the coronavirus pandemic, the availability of such virtual forms of communication may have saved the world from even greater disruption and calamity. Moreover, the unprecedented speed of COVID-19 vaccine development represented a remarkable triumph of disembodied globalization in the form of transnational data-sharing, global investment flows, and the utilization of global supply chains for the production of the vaccine. Unfortunately, the ensuing distribution of the vaccines suffered from *vaccine nationalism*. As global health experts have pointed out, the systematic efforts of wealthy countries in the Global North to reserve millions of doses for domestic use reinforced the long-standing inequalities in public health between the Global North and South.[22]

What seems largely missing in the theoretical framework of disjunctive globalization are concrete policy suggestions of how to counteract the negative impacts of desynchronized formations. It seems imperative to coordinate a worldwide realigning of the widening globalization cleavages. But the success of such an endeavor depends, in the first instance, on the enhancement of institutional capabilities to make the increasingly complex and differentiated dynamics of globalization work in a more synchronized and balanced manner that serves socially equitable ends. But even if national governments accepted the need to bridge the cleavages—by slowing down disembodied globalization and recharging the other formations—the actual implementation of pertinent polices would be immensely difficult. After all, the two principal mechanisms required to achieve this goal of readjustment—the strengthening of global solidarity and the creation of more effective institutions of global governance—face a steep uphill struggle under our current nationalist backlash conditions.

ECOLOGICAL GLOBALIZATION THEORIES

As we noted in chapter 4, postcolonial critics justifiably charged globalization theory with its complicity in the lack of epistemological pluralism inherent in Western knowledge systems. This problem also applies to their dominant conceptions of *nature*—a sphere habitually separated from *society*.[23] Defined in a nonbinary way, "nature" becomes *ecology*. This encompassing term refers to the practices, discourses, and materialities that cross the intersection of the artificially divided social and natural realms, including the important dimension of human engagement with and within nature. Such a nondualistic understanding of ecology suggests that the human body itself is an *ecological materiality*, just as it produces cultural meaning and serves as a medium for the extension of political power and economic management.[24]

As humans have globalized their impact upon Earth, their actions have become embedded into something as basic as geological rock formations. Whether it be in soot particles, radioactivity from nuclear bomb testing and plant spills, or plastic microfragments, the materiality of human activity is now being recorded on the skin of our planet. Thus, scientists who recognize the extended scope of recent global change accept that we now live in the *Anthropocene*. This concept names our present geological age during which our species has become a significant geophysical force acting on Earth's biosphere. Although the Anthropocene framework can be misused to defend the economic privileges of the Global North, it also helps us to conceive human existence and social change in the context of the compressed physical transformation of our planet. Social processes that go by the name of globalization can thus more easily be linked to planetary dynamics that constantly react to problems posed by the imbalance of the forces of which it is composed. To highlight the growing significance of the ecological dimension in our everyday existence, some social thinkers have suggested replacing the human-centered adjective *global* with *planetary*, which signifies much longer temporalities than the relatively short time of our species on Earth.[25]

Nearly two decades after its first explicit use by the chemistry Nobel laureate Paul Crutzen and the biologist Eugene Stoermer, Anthropocene has become a keyword that has appealed to the world with unusual force. Over the past decade, in particular, this foreboding sense of planetary complexity has touched all but the most hardened economic-growth advocates. Indeed, the scale and speed of human activities responsible for our home planet's ecological decline has been extreme. As a result, environmental issues such as global climate change and transboundary pollution have received much attention from research institutes, the media, politicians, economists, and the public in general. Unsustainable forms of ecological globalization are now recognized as threatening the very survival of life on Earth. Concerned observers have coined the term *ecocide* to characterize large-scale human acts that disrupt or destroy planetary ecosystems.[26] In recent years, a growing number of social thinkers utilize the ecocide framework to analyze multiple human-induced patterns of global environmental destruction, including the mass extinction of animal and plant species.

Still, the problems of climate change and environment deterioration have not yet informed globalization theory to the extent they should. Among the few exceptions among globalization thinkers is Eve Darian-Smith, whose work links ecological concerns to systemic patterns of social injustice such as exploitation, exclusion, violence, poverty, inequality, sexism, and racism. Combing a critical mode of theorizing with a strong focus on complexity, Darian-Smith starts the construction of her analytical framework of ecological globalization with a profound critique of what she calls *blinkered globalization theory*. What she means with this expression is that most mainstream globalization thinkers seem to be wearing blinkers when it comes to engaging with a wide range of critical scholarship and innovative social theory.[27]

In particular, Darian-Smith charges mainstream globalization theorists with failing to grapple with the enduring legacies of *environmental degradation* implemented over long histories of European colonialism and economies of extractive capitalism. In the spirit of constructive criticism, however, she offers what she considers to be the main reasons behind the blinkered thinking among mainstream theorists of globalization in the Euro-American academy.[28]

First, Darian-Smith notes that globalization theory in the Global North has historically emerged out of a state-centric

New Theories / 195

> **Eve Darian-Smith (1963–)** is Professor and department chair in Global and International Studies at the University of California, Irvine. She is an interdisciplinary scholar trained in law, history, politics, anthropology, and environmental studies. In addition to providing a comprehensive thematic and methodological overview of the transdisciplinary field of global studies, Darian-Smith's main contribution to globalization theory comes in the form of what might be called an intersectional model of ecological globalization. She argues that the immanent ecological collapse reflected in runaway climate change and other environmental challenges needs to be examined more thoroughly through the study of related neoliberal and neocolonial logics and unregulated processes of extractive capitalism in both the Global North and South. She also insists that theorizing about globalization has failed to foreground the profound relationality between humans and "more-than-human worlds." The latter expression refers to a world that both includes humans and exceeds humans, underscoring the complex interdependencies between all biological life on the planet.

analysis, which by the nature of its underlying Western modernist theories is often blind to alternative epistemologies—like those we discussed in the previous chapter in the context of postcolonialism and indigenous knowledge—that are not grounded in state territorial assumptions. As we noted in the introduction, most of what passes as mainstream social science relies on the production of empirical knowledge based on allegedly objective scientific data and apolitical analysis. However, such value-neutrality veils the intellectual conservatism that resists engaging with issues of power, privilege, and Eurocentrism. Moreover, the geospatial disconnect inherent in the dominant academic practices of methodological nationalism and scientific objectivity makes it easier for scholars in the Global North to pay little attention to the appalling manifestations of environmental degradation that often constitute the everyday reality in the poorer countries of the Global South.

Second, Darian-Smith points to the enduring lack of deep and broad transdisciplinary scholarship in the social sciences and humanities in the Euro-American academy that shields globalization theorists working in these fields from having to engage with environmental knowledges produced by earth-systems scholars, biologists, and climatologists. She concedes that such efforts would require much effort and professional funding, but the payoff would be the creation of holistic approaches to analyzing the complexity of *intersectional* ecological and social problems.

Third, Darian-Smith argues that the enduring bias toward economic domain thinking in globalization theory rooted in the neoliberal context of the 1990s and 2000s has stifled the necessary broadening of pertinent scholarship to address more systematically ecological and postcolonial concerns. Hence, much of globalization theory has overlooked the impact of global capitalism on the environment and the related disproportionate impacts on women, poor, indigenous, and racially marginalized communities. In particular, the pervasive economism in globalization theory has suppressed the emergence of innovative discourses in the Global North for transcending the human/nature binary that engages the key questions enabling the continued existence for human and other lifeforms in the face of today's immense *climate crisis*.

How, then, does Darian-Smith suggest to remedy these lingering inadequacies of globalization theory? Starting with the recognition that our collective future on this planet is one of *climate-driven globalization*, she argues that her ecological bottom line intersects with a host of related social justice issues. To illustrate her relational approach, Darian-Smith focuses on the unprecedented waves of wildfires that have swept across the planet in recent years. While these out-of-control blazes serve as just one measure of impending ecological disaster, they nonetheless help theorists to better understand how climate change is dramatically and disproportionately transforming a wide range of people's lives. Many of them live in the poor regions of the Global South and thus go unnoticed in mainstream consciousness and social media. In particular, *thinking through* this global calamity forces scholars and public intellectuals to engage with multiple worldviews that decenter Euro-American perspectives based on profit-maximizing capitalist imperatives. Hence, Darian-Smith assembles her alternative conceptual framework of ecological globalization theory by issuing an urgent call to her colleagues to develop and refine what some environmental thinkers refer to as a *planetary mode of thinking.*[29]

Applied to the analysis of global blazes driven by record-breaking world temperatures, this *new ecological style of inquiry* consists of three overlapping reflective procedures. The first activity amounts to *thinking about fires* in an empirical, data-driven way that expands our critical knowledge about why these blazes happen, whom they impact, and how they might be stopped.

Darian-Smith calls the second conceptual engagement *thinking with fires*, which seeks to overcome the *human/nature binary* that posits humans as the subject and fires as the object of study. Overcoming this dichotomy means recognizing the existential reality of our human lives being both within and part of nature through complex relationships that make up the web of life on Earth.

The third activity of this planetary style of inquiry manifests as *thinking through fires*, which opens new ways of transcending our conventional nation-bound worldviews and relations with each other. Highlighting fires as intercontinental phenomena blurring the boundaries between lands, seas, and atmospheres also sharpens our appreciation for postcolonial and indigenous worldviews rooted in deep understandings of existential interdependence that encourage *nonextractive* and *need-based economic practices*.

Finally, thinking through fires reveals the extent to which environmental degradation is linked to the political corrosion of liberal democracy. Spearheaded by national-populist leaders tied to corporate interests, the rolling back of environmental protections has become a hallmark of rising authoritarianism in the twenty-first century.[30]

Overall, then, Darian-Smith's call for integrating a planetary mode of thinking into globalization theory aims at bringing together the related problems of environmental destruction, social injustice, racism, antidemocracy, and Eurocentric systems of knowledge. The recent upswing of interest in climate change and other ecological issues among globalization scholars seems to indicate that there is a ray of hope on the horizon. Such growing efforts can go a long way toward the necessary erasure of the lingering shadows of ecocide and Eurocentric worldviews from globalization theory.

New Theories / 199

CONCLUDING REFLECTIONS ON THE FUTURE OF GLOBALIZATION THEORY

In this book, we considered major globalization theories crafted in *four principal modes of inquiry*. We assessed the strengths and weaknesses of each of these styles—*generalizing, domain, complexity*, and *critical thinking*—and explored some productive overlaps and intersections. We noted that globalization theorists have deeply challenged many prevailing ideas and practices in the social sciences and humanities. The resulting strengthening of the imperative to *globalize the research imagination* has put pressure on conventional academic landscapes and architectures shaped by methodological nationalism and Western-centric logics developed in the previous two centuries.

This task requires the integration and synthesis of multiple strands of knowledge in a way that does justice to the ever-growing complexity, fluidity, and connectivity of our globalizing world. Fortunately, mobilizing the global imaginary in this way has encouraged a new generation of globalization scholars to find innovative paths to move beyond these impasses, absences, and inherited ways of thinking that no longer resonate with the pressing global issues of our time.[31] In the closing paragraphs of this final chapter, then, let us indulge in a very brief speculation of how three intertwined tendencies in current globalization theory might develop in the foreseeable future.

The first trend relates to the domain mode of theorizing globalization. While scholarly examinations of single dimensions of globalization—especially its economic aspects—have dominated the field for decades, it has become increasingly obvious that such limited approaches no longer suffice in a world of increasing complexity. Hence, there has been a noticeable increase in domain studies that attempt to cut across multiple dimensions. Such a *broadening of domain thinking* indicates a renewed interest in generalizing styles of thinking. However, these forms of general theory tend to be less grandiose in their design and are thus tempered by a good dose of attention to existing complexities. The resulting hybridity of ways of thinking might result in a turn toward excessive abstraction, but it also boosts the development of transdisciplinary frameworks that offer multiple entry points to theorists located in different fields and eager to join the conversation.

The second related tendency impacting future trajectories of globalization theory is reflected in the *growing appeal of complexity thinking* in the social sciences and humanities. As we discussed in this chapter, the tremendous impact of digital technology on social relations, in particular, has prompted a new generation of globalization thinkers to build on existing conceptual models like the global network society to deepen our understanding of complex systems. Mirroring the turn to transdisciplinarity involved in multidimensional domain thinking, greater attention to complexity invites scholars to bridge the conventional boundaries between academic fields to provide a better picture of intricate emergent patterns of integration and rupture. As we noted in our discussion of Darian-Smith's intersectional model of ecological globalization, the recognition of intensifying complexity is the precondition for the formation of more diverse and inclusive frameworks of knowledge.

The third future trend is one of combining the growing academic attention to complexity and generalizing reasoning with Stage 2 types of *normative* critical inquiry we previously described as *socially and ecologically engaged theory*. Given that globalization theory is about conceptualizing social relations with a focus on transplanetary interdependencies, the descriptor "engaged" signals an intent to link explanatory with normative concerns. Engaged globalization theories are committed to making a positive difference in the everyday *glocal* lives of ordinary people. Moreover, they are engaged in the sense of nurturing a sensibility of *critical reflexivity* that comes with the recognition of the *historical specificity* of existing social arrangements. These critical perspectives seek to advance action-oriented interpersonal understandings while contesting various forms of domination, inequality, and injustice.

As we discussed in this book, the necessary task of reconfiguring and redesigning globalization theories must avoid being framed by Eurocentric themes and concerns and instead embrace the ethical imperative to negotiate transcultural codes for global engagement. Engaged globalization theories recognize and criticize global patterns of dominance emanating from the Global North and linked to escalating forms of ecological degradation. Thus, they acknowledge multiple manifestations of *difference*—and the terms on which difference is negotiated—as a key to improve our *common* human condition in a globalizing world. However, the academic goal of developing engaged *and* engaging theories of globalization goes beyond human-centered concerns. The main purpose of theory is not only to understand our world better, but to change it. The principal driving force behind this effort to bring about change should be the ethical intent to create better futures for *all sentient beings* on this wondrous planet.

NOTES

1. André C. Jordan, "De-Globalization: Fact or Fiction?," *Latin American Journal of Trade Policy* 12 (2022): 37–42.

2. Manfred B. Steger and Paul James, *Globalization Matters: Engaging the Global in Unsettled Times* (Cambridge, UK: Cambridge University Press, 2019). For a broader discussion of the "Great Unsettling," see Paul James and Manfred B. Steger, "Unsettling Subjectivity across Local, National, and Global Imaginaries: Producing an Unhappy Consciousness," *Glocalism: Journal of Culture, Politics and Innovation* no. 3 (2020), https://riviste.unimi.it/index.php/glocalism/article/view/20945.

3. Didem Buhari, "The Myth of Deglobalization: Definitional and Methodological Issues," in Manfred B. Steger, Roland Benedikter, Harald Pechlaner, and Ingrid Kofler, eds., *Globalization: Past, Present, Future* (Oakland: University of California Press, 2023), 74–89.

4. Rana Foroohar, *Homecoming: The Path to Prosperity in a Post-Global World* (New York: Crown, 2022), 26; Markus Kornprobst and Jon Wallace, "What is Deglobalization?," Chatham House, October 18, 2021, www.chathamhouse.org/2021/10/what-deglobalization.

5. Neil Dias Karunaratne, "The Globalization-Deglobalization Policy Conundrum," *Modern Economy* 3, no. 4 (2012): 373–83.

6. Walden Bello, *Deglobalization: Ideas for a New Economy* (London: Zed Books, 2004).

7. Matthew Louis Bishop and Anthony Payne, "The Political Economies of Different Globalizations: Theorizing Reglobalization," *Globalizations* 18, no. 1 (2021): 1–21; Matthew Bishop and Anthony Payne, *Reglobalization* (London: Routledge, 2021).

8. Peter A.G. Van Bergeijk, *Deglobalization 2.0: Trade and Openness during the Great Depression and the Great Recession* (Cheltenham, UK: Edward Elgar Publishing, 2019), 15.

9. Roland Wenzlhuemer, "Dis:connectivity in Global History," in Steger et. al., *Globalization: Past, Present, Future*, 11–26.

10. Roland Benedikter, "Re-Globalization: An Introductory Overview," in Roland Benedikter, Mirjam Gruber, and Ingrid Kofler, eds., *Re-Globalization: New Frontiers of Political, Economic, and Social Globalization* (Milton Park, UK: Routledge, 2022), 7–32.

11. Arjun Appadurai, "Disjuncture and Difference in the Global Cultural Economy," in Mike Featherstone, ed., *Global Culture: Nationalism and Modernity* (London: Sage, 1990), 295–310; Arjun Appadurai, *Modernity at Large: Cultural Dimensions of Globalization* (Minneapolis: University of Minnesota Press, 1996).

12. Manfred B. Steger and Paul James, "Disjunctive Globalization in the Era of the Great Unsettling," *Theory Culture & Society* 37, no. 7/8 (2020): 187–204.

13. Neil Selwyn, *What Is Digital Sociology?* (Cambridge, UK: Polity, 2019), 23–24; Elizabeth Kath, Julian H. Lee, and Aiden Warren, eds., *The Digital Global Condition* (Singapore: Springer Nature Singapore, 2023).

14. Daniele Schillirò, "Towards Digital Globalization and the COVID-19 Challenge," *International Journal of Business Management and Economic Research* 11, no. 2 (2020): 1711; Azeem Azhar, *The Exponential Age: How Accelerating Technology Is Transforming Business, Politics, and Society* (New York: Diversion Books, 2021), 232.

15. Klaus Schwab, *The Fourth Industrial Revolution* (Geneva: World Economic Forum, 2016); Bernard Marr, *Tech Trends in Practice: The 25 Technologies That Are Driving the 4th Industrial Revolution* (Chichester, UK: Wiley, 2020).

16. Azhar, *Exponential Age*, 15.

17. Richard Baldwin, *The Globotics Upheaval: Globalization, Robotics, and the Future of Work* (New York: Oxford University Press, 2019), 10, 139.

18. Nick Srnicek, *Platform Capitalism* (Cambridge, UK: Polity Press, 2017); Timothy E. Ström, *Globalization and Surveillance* (Lanham, MD: Rowman & Littlefield, 2019); Shoshanna Zuboff, *The Age of Surveillance Capitalism: The Fight for a Human Future at the New Frontier of Power* (New York: Public Affairs, 2019); Barrie Axford, "Where Globalities Are Made," *Global-e* 13, no. 12 (2020), www.21global.ucsb.edu/global-e/february-2020/where-globalities-are-made.

19. Steger and James, "Unsettling Subjectivity."

20. Paul James and Manfred B. Steger, "On Living in an Already-Unsettled World: COVID as an Expression of Larger Transformations," *Globalizations* 19, no. 3 (2022): 426–38.

21. Youngrong Lee, Ye Jin Jeon, Sunghyuk Kang, Jae Il Shin, Young-Chul Jung, and Sun Jae Jung, "Social Media Use and Mental Health during the COVID-19 Pandemic in Young Adults: A Meta-analysis of 14 Cross-sectional Studies," *BMC Public Health* 22, no. 995 (2022), https://doi.org/10.1186/s12889-022-13409-0; Nirmita Panchal, Heather Saunders, Robin Rudowitz, and Cynthia Cox, "The Implications of COVID-19 for Mental Health and Substance Use," *Kaiser Family*

Foundation, March 20, 2023, www.kff.org/coronavirus-covid-19/issue-brief/the-implications-of-covid-19-for-mental-health-and-substance-use/.

22. Yanqiu Rachel Zhou, "Vaccine Nationalism: Contested Relationships between COVID-19 and Globalization," *Globalizations* 19, no. 3 (2022): 454.

23. Bruno Latour, *We Have Never Been Modern* (Cambridge, MA: Harvard University Press, 1993).

24. Steger and James, *Globalization Matters*, 230–50.

25. Nigel Clark and Bronislaw Szerszynski, *Planetary Social Thought: The Anthropocene Challenge to the Social Sciences* (Cambridge, UK: Polity, 2021), 3–5, 93; Dipesh Chakrabarty, *The Climate of History in a Planetary Age* (Chicago: University of Chicago Press, 2021), 85–87.

26. Franz J. Broswimmer, *Ecocide: A Short History of the Mass Extinction of Species* (London: Pluto, 2002).

27. Eve Darian-Smith, "Academic Navel-Gazing: Debating Globalization as the Planet Burns," in Steger et al., *Globalization: Past, Present, Future*, 222–41.

28. Darian-Smith, 234–36.

29. Chakrabarty, *Climate of History*, 87; Clark and Szerszynski, *Planetary Social Thought*.

30. Eve Darian-Smith, *Global Burning: Rising Antidemocracy and the Climate Crisis* (Stanford, CA: Stanford University Press, 2022), 28–31, 133–37.

31. Jane Kenway and Johannah Fahey, eds., *Globalizing the Research Imagination* (London: Routledge, 2009), 4.

BRIEF GUIDE TO FURTHER READING

Since the modest beginnings of globalization theory in the 1990s, there has been a proliferation of literature on the subject. Many of these academic writings are not easily accessible to those who want to acquire some basic knowledge of the subject. However, readers who have digested the contents of this concise introduction should feel secure enough to advance more deeply into the thickets of globalization theory. The academic works listed below are meant as helpful stepping stones toward a fuller understanding of the field and related topics.

INTRODUCTION: WHAT IS GLOBALIZATION THEORY?

Barrie Axford's study, *Theories of Globalization* (Cambridge, UK: Polity, 2013) offers a full range of themes and arguments. Axford expertly combines his discussion of relevant theories with the presentation of his own insightful perspective. A more thinkers-centered approach that enhances readers' understanding of how their different ideas relate to each other can be found in Andrew Jones's readable book, *Globalization: Key Thinkers* (Cambridge, UK: Polity, 2010).

The two most accessible introductions to the growing transdisciplinary field of global studies can be found in Eve Darian-Smith and Philip C. McCarty, *The Global Turn: Theories, Research Designs, and Methods for Global Studies* (Oakland: University of California Press, 2017), and Manfred B. Steger and Amentahru Wahlrab, *What Is Global Studies? Theory and Practice* (London: Routledge, 2017).

For readers who want to delve more deeply into the history of globalization as well as learn about global history as an emerging subfield of history, I recommend Jürgen Osterhammel and Niels Petersson, *Globalization: A Very Short History* (Princeton, NJ: Princeton University Press, 2005); Nayan Chanda, *How Traders, Preachers, Adventurers and Warriors Shaped Globalization* (New Haven: Yale University Press, 2007); Sebastian Conrad, *What Is Global History?* (Princeton, NJ: Princeton University Press, 2017); and James Blaut, *The Colonizer's Model of the World: Geographical Diffusionism and Eurocentric History* (New York: Guilford Press, 2021).

CHAPTER 1: GENERAL THEORIES

In addition to the works discussed in this chapter, there are a number of foundational books that explore the tense relationship between globalization and various forms of modernity. Among these works are David Harvey, *The Condition of Postmodernity: An Enquiry into Origins of Cultural Change* (London: Basil Blackwell, 1989); Mike Featherstone, Scott Lash, and Roland Robertson, eds., *Global Modernities* (London: Sage, 1995); Arjun Appadurai, *Modernity At Large: Cultural Dimensions of Globalization* (Minneapolis: University of Minnesota Press, 1996); Ulrich Beck, *What Is Globalization?* (Cambridge, UK; Polity, 2000); Shmuel N. Eisenstadt, ed., *Multiple Modernities* (New Brunswick, NJ: Transaction Books, 2002); and Immanuel Wallerstein, *World-Systems Analysis: An Introduction* (Durham, NC: Duke University Press, 2004).

For readers interested in David Held's macro-mapping of globalization who want to familiarize themselves with more recent attempts, see Manfred B. Steger and Paul James, *Globalization Matters: Engaging the Global in Unsettled Times* (Cambridge, UK: Cambridge University Press, 2019).

Brief Guide to Further Reading / 207

CHAPTER 2: DOMAIN THEORIES

Comprehensive overviews of globalization theories related to the main domains discussed in this chapter include the following works:

Economics: Peter Dicken, *Global Shift: Mapping the Contours of the World Economy*, 7th ed. (New York: Guilford Press, 2015); and Dani Rodrik, *The Globalization Paradox: Democracy and the Future of the World Economy* (New York: W. W. Norton, 2012).

Politics: John Baylis and Steve Smith, *The Globalization of World Politics*, 8th ed. (Oxford, UK: Oxford University Press, 2020).

Culture: Mike Featherstone, ed., *Global Culture: Nationalism, Globalization and Modernity* (London: Sage, 1990); Victor Roudometof, *Glocalization: A Critical Introduction* (London: Routledge, 2016); and Jan Nederveen Pieterse, *Globalization and Culture: The Global Mélange*, 4th ed. (Lanham, MD: Rowman & Littlefield, 2019).

Ideology: Manfred B. Steger, *Globalisms: Facing the Populist Challenge* (Lanham, MD: Rowman & Littlefield, 2019).

CHAPTER 3: COMPLEXITY THEORIES

The most accessible introduction to both complexity theory and complexity science can be found in Melanie Mitchell, *Complexity: A Guided Tour* (Oxford, UK: Oxford University Press, 2011). More demanding treatments that have become classics in the field of complexity science include Fritjof Capra, *The Web of Life: A New Scientific Understanding of Living Systems* (New York: Anchor, 1996); and Ilya Prigogine, *The End of Certainty* (New York: The Free Press, 1997). A short but highly sophisticated introduction to the contemporary fluidity of globalization dynamics written from a social complexity perspective appears in Zygmunt Bauman, *Globalization: The Human Consequences* (New York: Columbia University Press, 1998).

CHAPTER 4: CRITICAL THEORIES

A brilliant and accessible introduction to the Critical Theory tradition of the German Frankfurt School can be found in Stephen Eric

208 / *Brief Guide to Further Reading*

Bronner, *Critical Theory: A Very Short Introduction* (Oxford, UK: Oxford University Press, 2017). Substantive discussions of critical globalization theories are available in Chamsy El-Ojeili and Patrick Hayden, eds., *Critical Theories of Globalization: An Introduction* (Houndmills, UK: Palgrave Macmillan, 2006); and Gary Browning, *Global Theory from Kant to Hardt and Negri* (Houndmills, UK: Palgrave Macmillan, 2011).

For readers searching for sensitive thematic and historical treatments of postcolonial and indigenous theories, I highly recommend Robert J.C. Young, *Postcolonialism: A Historical Introduction* (Malden, MA: Blackwell, 2001); Raewyn Connell, *Southern Theory: The Global Dynamics of Knowledge in Social Science* (Crow's Nest, New South Wales: Allen & Unwin, 2007); Boaventura de Souza Santos, *Epistemologies of the South: Justice against Epistemicide* (Boulder, CO: Paradigm Publishers, 2014); Julian Go, *Postcolonial Thought and Social Theory* (Oxford, UK: Oxford University Press, 2016); and Brenda Hokowhitu, Aileen Moreton-Robinson, Linda Tuhiwai-Smith, Chris Andersen, and Steve Larkin, eds., *Routledge Handbook of Critical Indigenous Studies* (New York: Routledge, 2022).

CHAPTER 5: NEW THEORIES

For an economically informed perspective on digital globalization, see Richard Baldwin, *The Great Convergence: Information Technology and the New Globalization.* (Cambridge: MA: Belknap Press, 2016); and Baldwin, *The Globotics Upheaval: Globalization, Robotics, and the Future of Work* (New York: Oxford University Press, 2019). An accessible treatment of the growing impact of digital technology on global social change can be found in Azeem Azhar, *The Exponential Age: How Accelerating Technology Is Transforming Business, Politics, and Society* (New York: Diversion Books, 2021).

An urgent warning of the unprecedented risks that AI and other fast-developing technologies pose to global order can be found in Mustafa Suleyman, *The Coming Wave: Technology, Power, and the 21st Century's Greatest Dilemma* (New York: Crown, 2023). For a more benign, neoliberal interpretation of the benefits of digitization, see Klaus

Brief Guide to Further Reading / 209

Schwab, *The Fourth Industrial Revolution* (Geneva: World Economic Forum, 2016). Timothy Ström offers a brilliant critique of this market-oriented perspective in his meticulously researched book, *Globalization and Surveillance* (Rowman & Littlefield, 2020). Erle C. Ellis provides a brief overview of the Anthropocene as both a concept and a geological age in his *Anthropocene: A Very Short Introduction* (Oxford, UK: Oxford University Press, 2018). A very readable discussion of the social impacts of the Anthropocene can be found in Clive Hamilton, *Defiant Earth: The Fate of Humans in the Anthropocene* (Cambridge, UK: Polity Press, 2017). More scholarly treatments that integrate various historical, philosophical, and sociological perspectives on the subject are reflected in in Dipesh Chakrabarty, *The Climate of History in a Planetary* Age (Chicago: University of Chicago Press, 2021); and Nigel Clark and Bronislaw Szerszynski, *Planetary Social Thought: The Anthropocene Challenge to the Social Sciences* (Cambridge, UK: Polity, 2021). For a short but sophisticated discussion of political dynamics in the context of the Anthropocene, see Bruno Latour, *Down to Earth: Politics in the New Climatic Regime* (Cambridge, Polity Press, 2018).

The most comprehensive treatment of the relationship between globalization and the environment is provided by Robyn Eckersley and Peter Christoff, *Globalization and the Environment* (Lanham, MD: Rowman & Littlefield, 2013). The book contains rich case studies and integrates policy-relevant issues.

INDEX

abductive thinking, 2
add-on effect, 99
al-Muqaddima, 25
Albrow, Martin: *The Global Age: State and Society beyond Modernity,* 39, 53–58, 121
Americanization, 91, 93, 98. *See also* cultural imperialism; westernization
analytical models, 42
Anders, William, 11
annihilation of space, 112
Anthropocene, 21, 171, 193. *See also* ecocide
Appadurai, Arjun, 172, 182–183, 206
Appelbaum, Richard, 152

Barber, Benjamin, 91, 93, 94
Baudrillard, Jean, 49
Behaim, Martin, 10
Bello, Walden, 178
billiard ball model of culture, 94
bits, 185
Blaut, James, 68

blinkered globalization theory, 173, 194
Bohm, David, 109,135
breadth, 14, 22–23, 29, 60
Buhari, Didem, 172, 176–180

Castells, Manuel: *The Information Age,* 106–107, 118–127, 129–132; global network society, 107, 119, 121–123, 125–127, 130, 131–132, 186, 188, 200
centers, 119. *See also* hubs
civilizations, 93–94. *See also* clash of civilizations
clashing cultural differences, 32, 73
clash of civilizations, 93–94, 98
clear scientific propositions, 138
climate crisis, 196
climate-driven globalization theory, 173, 197
colonial matrix of power, 161–164
coloniality, 162–164; of knowledge, 162; of power, 161–164. *See also* decoloniality

colonizer's model of the world, 68
Columbus, Christopher, 10
complex adaptive systems (CAS), 110
complexity, 106–113, 115, 118–120, 122–123, 125–135, 167, 172, 180–183, 196, 199, 200; as a mode of theorizing, 30, 106–107, 112–113, 125; definition of, 108; in global interconnectivity, 108; in systems theory, 109–110; in interdependent dynamics of natural and social systems, 108
connectivity, 18–19, 28. *See also* interconnectivity
Consequences of Modernity, The, 49. *See also* Giddens, Anthony
conservatism, 15
contingently, 109
Copernicus, Nicolaus, 10–11
core, 78
cosmopolitan world, 14
critical, 33, 36, 136–141, 149–168, 200–202; globalization theory, 139, 152–153, 155–156, 166; reflexivity, 201; theories, 30, 33, 138, 143–144, 152; theories of globalization, 152; theory, 5, 59, 138, 142–144, 159, 164; thinking, 33, 132, 140–143, 150, 156, 158, 163–164, 166–167; thinking framework, 140
crossovers, 154–155
cultural, 70, 72, 89–98; difference, 32, 73, 90, 92–94, 96–98; differentialism, 92–93, 97; globalization, 32, 73, 90–91, 93–98; imperialism, 91, 93, 98; relations, 75
cyberspace, 112, 125, 173–174, 189

Darian-Smith, Eve, 173, 194–200, 206; an intersectional model of

ecological globalization, 195; blinkered globalization theory, 194; environmental degradation, 194;
decentering, 41, 156–157
decisional, 60
decolonization process, 159, 163. *See also* decoloniality
decoloniality, 163, 165. *See also* decolonization process
deductive thinking, 2
deglobalization, 34, 172–174, 176–181; effects of 2008 Global Financial Crisis, 174; implications of COVID-19 pandemic, 175; influence of nationalist-populist forces, 174; linked to economic nationalism, 174; relationship to Great Recession and Eurozone Crisis, 174.
delinking, 178–179
denationalization, 28, 85
depth, 23, 60
deterritorialization, 20, 85–89, 94, 112, 117, 145–146, 148; absolutists, 85–86; relativists, 86, 88
dewesternization, 163
digital, 107, 118–124, 131; digitization, 34, 132, 172, 176, 184–185, 188–189; digitized, 184
globalization, 188–189, 191
disembedding, 52; institutions, 52, 65; mechanisms, 52
disembodied globalization, 184, 187, 191–192
disjointed, 12, 172, 181–184
disjunctive globalization theory, 172, 181–182, 191
distanciation, 51–52
distributive, 60
divided self, 190

Index / 213

domain, 73, 83, 88, 99, 103, 172, 179, 182–183, 189, 196, 199–200; theories, 30–32, 72, 84, 98; theory, 39, 72–73
Durkheim, Émile, 25–26, 32, 43, 46, 64

Earthrise, 11, 20
ecocide, 21, 194, 198
ecological materiality, 192
ecology, 58–59, 75, 192
economic dimension of globalization, 75
economic nationalism, 174
economic relations, 72, 75, 77, 150
Einstein, Albert, 40, 108
Eisenstadt, Shmuel, 66
emancipatory, 4–5, 22, 97, 139, 143, 152, 155, 163, 166–167; challenge existing social systems, 5; global justice movement, 139; social movements, 166; social change, 167; ways of theorizing, 22
embodied globalization, 184, 188
emergent process, 180
Empire, 88–89
engaged theory of globalization, 183
environmental degradation, 83, 194, 196, 198
epistemicide, 158
epistemologies, 157–158, 195
epochal shift, 28, 53, 79
ethnoscapes, 182
evidence, 3
explanatory, 145, 147–148, 201
exponential technologies, 187
extensity, 60, 62–63, 144, 186, 188

fact, 4
fascism, 15, 83
finanscapes, 182

finitude, 56
flows, 6, 13, 20–21, 23, 60–61, 75, 79, 112, 120, 123
folly of globalization theory, 147
form, 184. See also formation
form of consciousness, 13
formation, 184, 187–189, 191–193, 200
four principal modes of inquiry, 199
four social formations of globalization, 183
Fourth Industrial Revolution, 186
free markets, 76, 178
free trade, 12, 15, 76
Friedman, Milton, 15
Friedman, Thomas, 72, 77–79, 81

general, 32, 38–40, 42–43, 45, 48–49, 53, 57–59, 63–64, 67–69, 100, 126, 131–133, 164, 167, 182–183, 199–200; theories, 30–31, 38–41; Theory of Employment, Interest, and Money (1936), 40; Theory of Relativity, 38; theory, 37–42, 66, 69
geographic origin, 64–65
Germinal Phase, 47
Giddens, Anthony: *The Conse-quences of Modernity*, 38–39, 49–53, 55–58, 64–67, 145
Gita, Bhagavad, 140
global, 6–22, 47, 52–54, 56, 74, 78–83, 95–96, 104–134, 137, 150–155, 170; Age, 13, 39, 53–54, 113, 125, 127, 159; capitalism approach, 79; cities, 106, 114–117, 124–125; cities model, 116–117; citizenship, 139, 155–156; city, 115, 133; civil society, 7, 84; complex-ity, 107, 111, 123, 127–134; economy, 14, 55, 76, 80–81, 114, 117, 121, 132, 174, 179; fluids (GFs), 21, 107,

214 / *Index*

global *(continued)*
129–130, 134; governance
structures, 84, 177; history, 48,
161, 206; hybrids, 127–128, 130, 133;
imaginary, 6, 8, 10, 15–16, 18,
20–21, 85, 199; justice movement,
16, 139, 151–152, 176; literacy, 155;
mélange, 95–96, 167; network
society, 33, 107, 119, 121–123,
125–127, 130, 132–133, 186, 188, 200;
police state, 83; problems, 14, 56,
69, 133–134, 155, 171, 181; scale, 7, 13,
42, 81, 84, 113, 115; value chains
(GVCs), 81–82, 187; village, 11, 20,
112, 133
Global Financial Crisis (2008), 76,
172, 174
globalisation, 52
globalism, 8, 15–18, 55, 85, 145,
161–162
globality, 8, 13–14, 18, 39, 54–57, 86,
111, 117, 129, 148, 189
globalization-from-above, 151
globalization-from-below, 151
globalization/coloniality, 163
globalizing, 48–64, 70; capitalism
and, 72; modernity linked with,
49, 53, 65; tendencies of, 53, 65
globally integrated networks
(GINs), 107, 128, 133–134
globaloney, 144
globe, 9, 10, 21, 44, 51–53, 55–56, 75,
89, 150. *See also* globus
globotics upheaval, 187
globus, 9–10
glocal, 8, 12, 18, 53, 114, 118, 201;
contexts, 106,
glocalization, 12, 46, 98, 116, 133
grand theory, 32, 42, 132, 164
Great Powers, 175
Great Unsettling, 172, 176, 181, 184,
190

Hardt, Michael, 72, 88–89, 127
Harvey, David: theory of the
spatial fix, 115–116, 132
Hawking, Stephen, 108
Held, David: general globalization
theory, 39, 57–63, 68, 167, 186, 206
heterogeneity, 90
historical specificity, 201
historicism, 154
homo sapiens, 68
homogeneity, 90, 93
horizontal integration, 47
hubs, 117, 125. *See also* centers
human/nature binary, 196–197
Huntington, Samuel: clash of
civilizations, 93–94
hybrid, 32, 66, 73, 89, 94–98, 111–112,
127–128, 130, 133, 200; challenges
to cultural matters in, 96; global
forms of, 127; hybridization,
process of, 32; hybridity
thinking in, 97; hybridizing
global culture and, 89; translocal identities and, 96
hyperglobalizers, 27–28, 30, 59

ideology, 15, 54, 59, 149, 174
ideoscapes, 182
imagination, 18, 20, 22, 69, 141, 181
impact propensity, 60
implosion of space, 112
'ilm-al'umran, 25
Incipient Phase, 47
inclusion versus exclusion, 120
index, 22–23
Indigenous peoples, 63; local forms
of knowledge and, 157–159;
theoretical approaches to, 64,
139, 150, 156–158, 164, 183, 195;
traditional knowledge systems
of, 150, 198; transnational
resistance networks of, 151

Index / 215

inductive thinking, 2
Industrial Age, 121, 124
inequalities, 16, 139, 191
Information Age, 119, 121–124, 126,
133. *See also* Castells, Manuel
informational capitalism, 122
infrastructures, 60, 80, 82, 110,
188–189
institutionalization: dimensions of
global, 184; forms of, 60;
structural mechanisms of, 60
intensifying cultural sameness,
32, 73
intensity, 60–63, 144, 186
International relations theory (IR
theory), 7, 177
interpretation, 4, 12, 172, 208
intersectional, 195–196, 200

James, Paul, 172, 183–187, 189–190
jihad, 17, 93, 98
justice globalism, 15–17

Keynes, John Maynard, 40. *See also*
Keynesianism
Keynesianism, 41, 76
Khaldūn, Ibn, 24–25

Levitt, Theodore, 72, 77, 79
liberalism, 15, 50,
lingua franca, 92, 165
localization, 179
logic, 3
long-term cyclical process, 44
Lovelock, James, 11
Lyotard, François, 49

Macro-level theories, 3
Magellan, Ferdinand, 10
manage complexity, 122
market globalism, 15–17
Marx, Karl, 25, 32, 43, 64, 146

McDonaldization, 91–92, 98. *See
also* McWorld
McLuhan, Marshall, 112
McWorld, 91–93. *See also*
McDonaldization
McWorld versus Jihad, 93
mediascapes, 182
Merton, Robert K., 74
methodologies: forms of globalism
in, 7, 85, 145; glocalism in, 7, 107;
nationalism and, 7, 85, 132, 145,
196, 199
Micro-level theories, 3
Mid-range theories, 3
middle-range theory, 74
Mignolo, Walter, 139, 160–164
Mills, C. Wright, 42
minimal phase model of globalization, 47
Mittelman, James H., 139, 152–157
mobility, 18, 20–21, 29, 33, 45, 59,
68–69, 79, 98, 108, 121, 123, 128, 187,
189–190
modality framework, 30–31
modernity: age of, 53–56; colonial
dimensions of, 161, 163; critical
approaches to, 161; theoretical
perspectives on, 8, 13, 25–26,
32–33, 38–39, 41, 47, 49–58, 64–66,
78, 84, 93, 100, 135, 139, 146,
160–163. *See also* modern
world-system
modern world-system, 27. *See also*
modernity
modernity/coloniality, 161, 163. *See
also* modernity/coloniality
critical school of thought
modes: forms of interaction in, 61;
networked relationships of, 127;
theoretical approaches to, 5,
30–31, 41. *See also* modality
modality, 30–31. *See also* modes

216 / *Index*

multiscalar, 111, 114, 121, 133
multicausal process, 59
multicentric, 68
multidirectional, 68, 119, 123, 161
multidisciplinarity, 100–101
multidisciplinary, 6, 99–102, 175
multipolarity, 163, 176
multus, 101

national imaginary, 20–21, 85
nature, 192, 195–198
need-based economic practices, 198
Negri, Antonio, 72, 88–89
neo-isms, 15
neoliberal power elites, 15
Neoliberalism, 15, 76, 156
network: dimensions of power in, 119, 126; enterprises and, 121, 133; global society and, 21, 33, 107, 119, 121–123, 125–127, 130, 132–133, 186, 188, 200; mechanisms of state control in, 87; theoretical approaches to, 7, 13, 18–20, 32–33, 107, 117–134. *See also* systems
network theory of power, 126
networking power, 126
network power, 126
networked power, 126
network-making power, 126
new ecological style of inquiry, 197
nodes, 119–121, 123–125, 128
non-extractive, 198

objective: dimensions of reality in, 4; forms of globalization and, 184, 187–188, 190; theoretical perspectives on, 3
objective reality, 4. *See also* objective
offshoring, 14

Ohmae, Kenichi, 85
one world, 14
organizational dimensions, 60–61, 68
orientalism, 157
outcome, 147, 151, 153
outsource manufacturing jobs, 80. *See also* outsourcing
outsourcing, 14. *See also* outsource manufacturing jobs

Parsons, Talcott, 42, 46, 52
paradigms, 2, 5, 41–42, 102, 150
particles and waves, 130
patterns, 5
periphery, 29, 78
Pieterse, Jan Nederveen, 41, 66, 73, 94–96, 167
planet-wide, 113
planetary consciousness, 65
planetary mode of thinking, 197–198
platform capitalism, 189
pluriversality, 163
political and governmental relations, 75
postcolonial theory, 157, 161. *See also* postcolonial and indigenous theory
postcolonial and indigenous theory, 64, 139. *See also* postcolonial theory
posthuman, 189
postmodern age, 50
presentism, 66–67
public intellectuals, 142, 165, 197

qualitative attributes, 7, 18. *See also* qualitatively
qualitatively, 80. *See also* qualitative attributes
quantitative, 80

quantitative measurements, 7, 22, 24,
quantum theorists, 108

re-empowerment of the local and national, 178
Reagan, Ronald, 16
reflexivity, 52, 55, 122, 141, 153, 166. *See also* critical reflexivity
refutability, 4
regional integration, 146
regional phenomenon, 139
reglobalization, 172, 180–181
relational, 108–109, 158, 195, 197
religious globalism, 15–17
Republic, 140
Ritzer, George, 91–91
Robertson, Roland, 38, 45–49, 66–67
Robinson, William, 72, 78–82, 87, 100–101, 152, 167
Rosenberg, Justin, 138, 144–148, 164

Santa Fe Institute, 110
Santos, Boaventura de Sousa, 139, 158–159
Sassen, Saskia, 106, 113–118, 121, 124, 132, 145, 167
scapes, 20, 182
Scholte, Jan Aart, 72, 86–89, 145, 166
scientific method, 2–3, 65, 140
semiperiphery, 27
shrinkage of space, 112
skeptics, 27–28, 30, 59, 135, 145
social condition, 13–14, 147–148
social Darwinism, 26
social distancing, 175, 190
social imaginaries, 20–21, 182
social injustices, 33, 139
social meanings, 4, 13
social stratification, 32, 43, 61, 87

socially and ecologically engaged theory, 200
society, 192
sovereignty, 7, 28, 32, 72, 83–85, 87–89, 145, 177
space of flows, 21, 123, 125, 130
space of places, 123
spatial, 7, 9, 13–14, 20–21, 24
spatial complexities, 116
spatialization of time, 112
specific dated events, 44
sphaira, 9
stages, 2, 26–27, 32. *See also* waves
Steger, Manfred B., 172, 183–187, 189–190
strategic transformations, 155
structural, 60, 67; adjustment programs, 82; functionalism, 25, 42
structure versus agency problem, 134
Struggle-for-Hegemony Phase, 47
sub-global, 113–114
subduing space, 112
superconductor for global capitalism, 86
supraterritoriality, 13, 20, 86
surveillance capitalism, 189
synchronization, 19
systems, 1, 5, 11–12, 15–16, 20, 26, 31, 35; theory, 107–108; systemic expulsions, 116

Take-Off Phase, 47, 66
technological relations, 75
technoscapes, 182
terra mobilis, 21
territoriality, 32, 57, 72, 83–85, 177
Thatcher, Margaret, 16
theoria, 1
theorist, 2
theorizing, 2

theory, 1, 2; spatial fix, 115
thick description, 150
thinking about fires, 197
thinking through, 197
thinking through fires, 198
thinking with fires, 197
Third World, 48, 163
three camps model, 29
three waves, 29
ties, 119, 121, 130
time-space compression, 20
time-space distanciation, 51–52
timeless time, 21, 124–125, 133
totalizing discourse, 54
transdisciplinarity, 101–102, 154, 200
transformationalists, 27, 29, 30, 59
transnational capital, 14, 79–83
transnational capitalist class
    (TCC), 14, 81–82
transnational state apparatus
    (TNS), 81–82
transworld instantaneity, 19, 86
transworld simultaneity, 19, 86
Type 1: thick globalization, 61–62
Type 2: diffused globalization,
    61–62
Type 3: expansive globalization,
    62–63
Type 4: thin globalization, 61–62
typology of globalization, 61

umma, 16
Uncertainty Phase, 48, 67
unhappy consciousness, 173, 190
unreality of place, 112

urban spaces, 106
Urry, John, 107, 127–132, 135

vaccine nationalism, 191
value-free, 4, 140–141
velocity, 60, 62–63, 186
vertical, 114–115, 117. *See also*
    vertical integration
vertical integration, 46. *See also*
    vertical
violence of abstraction, 41, 68

Waldseemüller, Martin, 10
waves, 27–29, 90, 130. *See also* stages
waves of deglobalization model,
    179
Weber, Max, 25–26, 32, 43, 52, 64,
    146
Werner Heisenberg, 109
westernization, 91–92, 98. *See also*
    Americanization
Whole Earth Catalogue, 12
world economy, 14, 27, 78, 80, 116,
    120, 138, 148, 179
world interdependence, 65
World Social Forum (WSF), 16, 151
world-system, 27, 78. *See also*
    modern world-system
world-systems theory, 27, 78–79.
    See also modern world-system;
    world-system

Zapatista Army of National
    Liberation, 151
Zapatista Solidarity Network, 151

Founded in 1893,
UNIVERSITY OF CALIFORNIA PRESS
publishes bold, progressive books and journals
on topics in the arts, humanities, social sciences,
and natural sciences—with a focus on social
justice issues—that inspire thought and action
among readers worldwide.

The UC PRESS FOUNDATION
raises funds to uphold the press's vital role
as an independent, nonprofit publisher, and
receives philanthropic support from a wide
range of individuals and institutions—and from
committed readers like you. To learn more, visit
ucpress.edu/supportus.

www.ingramcontent.com/pod-product-compliance
Ingram Content Group UK Ltd.
Pitfield, Milton Keynes, MK11 3LW, UK
UKHW042337250425
457898UK00002B/87